TRAIN TO TRI:

Your First Triathlon

TRAIN TO TRI:
Your First Triathlon

Linda Cleveland and Kris Swarthout

HUMAN KINETICS

Library of Congress Cataloging-in-Publication Data
Names: Cleveland, Linda, 1977- | Swarthout, Kris. | USA Triathlon.
Title: Train to tri : your first triathlon / USA Triathlon with Linda
  Cleveland and Kris Swarthout.
Description: Champaign, IL : Human Kinetics, [2017] | Includes index.
Identifiers: LCCN 2017012974 (print) | LCCN 2016058925 (ebook) | ISBN
  9781492536932 (ebook) | ISBN 9781492536741 (print)
Subjects: LCSH: Triathlon--Training.
Classification: LCC GV1060.73 (print) | LCC GV1060.73 .T73 2017 (ebook) | DDC
  796.42/57--dc23
LC record available at https://lccn.loc.gov/2017012974

ISBN: 978-1-4925-3674-1 (print)

This publication is written and published to provide accurate and authoritative information relevant to the subject matter presented. It is published and sold with the understanding that the author and publisher are not engaged in rendering legal, medical, or other professional services by reason of their authorship or publication of this work. If medical or other expert assistance is required, the services of a competent professional person should be sought.

The web addresses cited in this text were current as of December 2016, unless otherwise noted.

Acquisitions Editor: Michelle Maloney; **Developmental Editor:** Laura Pulliam; **Managing Editor:** Caitlin Husted; **USA Triathlon Editors:** Jayme McGuire and Chuck Menke; **Copyeditor:** Bob Replinger; **Indexer:** Alisha Jeddeloh; **Cover Designer:** Kelsey Couts/USA Triathlon; **Photograph (cover):** Rich Cruse/USA Triathlon; **Photographs (interior):** © Human Kinetics, unless otherwise noted; **Photo Asset Manager:** Laura Fitch; **Visual Production Assistant:** Joyce Brumfield; **Photo Production Manager:** Jason Allen; **Senior Art Manager:** Kelly Hendren; **Illustrations**: © Human Kinetics; **Printer:** Versa Press

Human Kinetics books are available at special discounts for bulk purchase. Special editions or book excerpts can also be created to specification. For details, contact the Special Sales Manager at Human Kinetics.

Printed in the United States of America   10 9 8 7 6 5 4 3 2 1

The paper in this book is certified under a sustainable forestry program.

Human Kinetics
Website: www.HumanKinetics.com

United States: Human Kinetics
P.O. Box 5076
Champaign, IL 61825-5076
800-747-4457
e-mail: info@hkusa.com

Canada: Human Kinetics
475 Devonshire Road Unit 100
Windsor, ON N8Y 2L5
800-465-7301 (in Canada only)
e-mail: info@hkcanada.com

Europe: Human Kinetics
107 Bradford Road
Stanningley
Leeds LS28 6AT, United Kingdom
+44 (0) 113 255 5665
c-mail: hk@hkeurope.com

I dedicate this book to my amazing children, Isaac and Olivia. Your smiles and laughter bring joy to my life.

—*Linda*

I dedicate this book to my wife Jill; my children Stephanie, Col, Julian, and London; and my entire family. Without their love and support, I would never have been able to become who I am today.

—*Kris*

CONTENTS

ACKNOWLEDGMENTS

I would like to acknowledge my coauthor, Kris. We enjoyed working together on this project. We complemented each other's writing and worked tirelessly to meet every deadline on time. Thanks! I also appreciate USA Triathlon's support of me during this project.

—*Linda*

I would like to acknowledge all the athletes and coaches who have influenced, supported, and guided me through my life and career. I would also like to tip my hat to my coauthor, Linda, who has been my "bestie" for many years. I hope we'll be friends forever.

—*Kris*

INTRODUCTION

Welcome to *Train to Tri: Your First Triathlon*. Triathlon is a relatively new sport. A rapid increase in events and technology has emerged in the last 15 years. Statistics show that beginner triathletes who are participating in sprint- and standard-distance triathlons have been at the forefront of this rise. With this rapid growth comes change in how best to train for a triathlon. Now more than ever, triathletes just starting in the sport need a clear, detailed training resource. A plethora of sources of information is available both in print and on the Internet; the problem is trying to decipher what is best for you.

If you are a first-time participant in a sprint-distance event, you cannot adapt an Ironman-distance training plan and hope for the best. You need a resource that can help you tune out the noise and give you clear and concise information and guidance. This book is that source. Some readers may not currently be physically active, whereas others may already be running, cycling, or swimming as a way to stay fit. This book caters to both groups. It is not intended to teach a new triathlete how to finish an Ironman-distance event; rather, it is designed to educate and guide a beginner athlete safely to and through a sprint- or standard-distance triathlon.

In this book we break down proper training techniques for all aspects of the sport. We discuss various training methodologies and help you go from simply working out to training. Example training plans will guide you to race day, and we show you how to modify and personalize those plans to fit your particular needs and lifestyle parameters. Triathlon training is about more than just swimming, biking, and running, and for that we break down nutrition, race selection, choosing a training group, equipment, strength training, and race-day execution. All this may seem daunting right now, but that is why you have this book. Let it guide you all the way to the postrace celebration. Let's look at what's inside.

Chapter 1: Taking the Triathlon Readiness Assessment

We start with a chapter that includes a detailed questionnaire for you to complete. You will answer questions about age, body mass index, fitness history, available training time, and medical issues. The answer to each question helps assign you to a fitness level: bronze (suboptimal), silver (intermediate), or gold (optimal). By tallying the answers to all these questions, you will be able to assess your baseline triathlon fitness and start thinking about the appropriate training plan for your race. This chapter also explains and defines common terminology that is used and referred to throughout the book. The chapter addresses training time requirements normally associated with each of the common distances of triathlon. We show you how you can balance your nonathletic time with physical training and still be able to achieve your goal. We explain that training for a triathlon is a commitment and that attempting to cut corners can lead to negative results, including, but not limited to, injuries and a failure to reach your goal. We also discuss how satisfying it is when all your training, hard work, good nutrition, and tapering leads to the accomplishment of finishing your first triathlon.

Chapter 2: Choosing Your First Race

In this chapter we describe the various kinds of triathlons, distances, and race environments (on-road versus off-road) and the importance of signing up for a race that suits your abilities. You will be guided by your fitness scores from chapter 1. For example, if you have just become interested in fitness (bronze level), you would want to choose a sprint as your first race distance rather than an Ironman. If you are more active (silver level), you may start with a sprint-distance race and quickly move to a standard-distance event. We make a clear disclaimer that if you are looking to go from beginner to Ironman, this is not the book for you. We focus on sprint- and standard-distance events only.

Chapter 3: Gearing Up

Because triathlon is a combination of three sports, a bewildering amount of gear is available for training and competition. This chapter helps you separate the must-have gear from the nice-to-have gear. It is divided into sections for swimming, cycling, running, and miscellaneous training equipment (foam rollers, heart rate monitors, and so on). Within each section, equipment is listed roughly from most essential to optional. For each piece of equipment we recommend desirable features and give suggested price ranges.

Chapter 4: Your Triathlon Support Group

As with any undertaking requiring months of planning and commitment, you can benefit from having support when preparing for your first triathlon. This chapter discusses groups that can help you attain your goals. Most of you likely have a nearby cycling, running, or triathlon club that can provide motivation and advice. Although these groups can be beneficial, we caution you that group workouts should coordinate with your personal triathlon training goals. Finally, we discuss ways to integrate your training with the rest of your life and obtain support from spouses, loved ones, and employers.

Chapter 5: Swimming

Swimming may be intimidating to first-time triathletes, and it is often the weakest link in their first race. This chapter is packed with swim technique drills to help the novice triathlete experience success in the water. Also discussed is how to overcome the fear of open-water swimming. We outline how to plan a swim workout rather than just swim, how to correct common stroke mechanics errors, and how to take your swim workouts on the road when you are traveling. This chapter dives deep into common technique training and helps the first-timer avoid wasting hours in the pool, lake, or ocean. It concludes with information on how to exit the water effectively and transition to the bike.

Chapter 6: Cycling

The chapter focuses on instructions and drills to foster proper bike technique and skill development. Step-by-step instructions show you how to make common, on-the-fly repairs for mishaps such as flat tires and dropped chains. We also discuss when you should seek an expert to make more difficult repairs. The chapter closes by welcoming you back to the transition rack.

Chapter 7: Running

This chapter discusses the dynamics of transitioning from bike to run. Both run cadence and brick training sessions will give you a clear picture of what it is like to go from biking to running from a physical exertion standpoint. Brick training is defined and emphasized, and we explain how and when it should be implemented into a training plan. Run technique, skill development, and classic running workouts are explained.

Chapter 8: Strength and Flexibility

Any successful triathlete knows that good triathlon preparation is more than just swimming, cycling, and running. Good strength and flexibility are key to improving triathlon performance and staying injury free. Triathlon-specific strength and flexibility sessions are essential components to the training plans in chapters 10 and 11. We give step-by-step instructions with photos for our favorite strength exercises. We also explain how strength training should progress with the triathlete's season and physical development. In addition, we give safety tips and recommendations for those new to strength and flexibility workouts.

Chapter 9: Nutrition and Rest

Proper nutrition and rest are essential but often-overlooked components of training plans. Beginning triathletes may not be aware of the body's increased need for fuel and fluids during training and competition. This chapter teaches you how to fuel your increased activity with healthy food and water. We discuss the need to fuel before, during, and after training. The chapter concludes with a discussion of rest and recovery as key components to the training plans presented in the following two chapters. We explain why more training isn't always better and why sufficient rest and recovery (including tapering) is the key to making periodized training plans work. We discuss how to listen to your body and detect symptoms of overtraining that can lead to burnout and injuries.

Chapter 10: Sprint-Distance Triathlon Training Plans

Sprint triathlon distances may vary, but they typically comprise a 750-meter swim, a 20-kilometer bike ride, and a 5-kilometer run. Before presenting the week-by-week training schedules, we provide detailed descriptive information and examples about following the plans. Triathlon training plans in other books for beginners have been criticized as being too complex and difficult. In this book the plans are clear and easy to follow, even for novice triathletes. All training plans incorporate the usual training phases, from base building to tapering. We include training plans for bronze, silver, and gold levels with options to individualize those plans along the way.

Chapter 11: Standard-Distance Triathlon Training Plans

Standard-distance triathlons (previously known as Olympic-distance triathlons) comprise a 1,500-meter swim (nearly a mile), a 40-kilometer bike ride, and a 10-kilometer run. This chapter uses the same format as the previous chapter does, presenting week-by-week training plans for bronze, silver, and gold levels. Detailed information and examples show you how to use the tables and how to depart from the prescribed workout when necessary.

Chapter 12: Preparing to Race

This chapter spells out the final preparations in the weeks, days, and hours leading up to the big race. We then discuss the benefits of tapering and appropriate methods to use according to race distance, as well as what you can expect to feel like during your taper. This chapter includes important tips and checklists on getting to the event, scouting the course, what to bring, what to eat (or avoid!) before a race, and settling prerace nerves. It includes some easy-to-follow advice about how to get a wetsuit on, how zip laces save time in transition, how to find your bike in transition, and so on.

Chapter 13: Your Race-Day Experience

This chapter describes in detail what to expect between the start and finish of your race, including mental success strategies. We cover the swim start and dealing with the frenzy of flailing arms and legs. Next, we give details on how to find and mount your bike in the transition area and then maintain a sustainable gear and cadence throughout the bike segment. Then we give tips on making a smooth transition from cycling to running. Finally, we discuss pacing strategies for the final run.

Chapter 14: Assessing Your Performance

This chapter encourages you to assess your performance in your first triathlon: Did you have any specific problems during the race? Was your pacing correct? Were you able to finish strong without thinking that you raced too conservatively? This chapter also provides information about recovery and guidelines about when you might start training for another race. In addition, we offer information on goal setting and building on your triathlon success.
We conclude by encouraging you to try another triathlon and perhaps make it a lifelong pursuit!

This book serves as a guide and resource to help the first-time triathlete train for and complete a first sprint- or standard-distance race. It is an absolute must-have resource for anyone thinking about getting into triathlon. The book is full of useful information for the first-time triathlete including training plans, techniques, nutrition tips, equipment advice, and race-day strategies. We hope that anyone, from fitness enthusiasts to those who are ready to start exercising, will gain insight into what it takes to train for and complete a triathlon. We hope you enjoy the book!

PART I

ASSESSING YOUR TRIATHLON READINESS

CHAPTER 1

TAKING THE TRIATHLON READINESS ASSESSMENT

Triathlon is a popular and fast-growing sport. USA Triathlon (USAT) now has more than 150,000 members. USAT has sanctioned more than 35,000 races over the past 30 years and has certified over 2,500 coaches. The numbers continue to rise. People decide to do triathlons for a variety of reasons, such as living a healthier and more active lifestyle, losing weight, eating better, learning how to swim, learning how to bike, learning how to run, getting stronger, and being a good role model. Regular exercise has been shown to combat disease by lowering blood pressure, lowering cholesterol, improving mood, reducing weight, boosting energy, promoting better sleep, and putting a spark in your step. We know that every reader is different, so we won't prescribe a one-size-fits-all training plan. We want to prepare you to complete your first triathlon so that you can feel the sense of achievement of becoming a real triathlete and claiming those bragging rights!

To get a sense of where you are fitness- and experience-wise, let's start with a questionnaire for you to complete. We call this the Triathlon Readiness Assessment (TRA). The TRA asks you questions about your age, body mass index, fitness history, available training time, and medical issues. Be honest with your answers based on your current state; skewing your answers toward where you want to be versus where you are will start you at a level that is too aggressive and will not help you reach the goal of successfully preparing for your first triathlon. The answers to each question in the TRA will assign you to a fitness level: bronze, silver, or gold. The bronze fitness level group is the beginner group. In this group, you will focus on building base fitness and endurance; work specifically on skills and techniques in the swim, bike, and run; and spend most of your time training to complete the race distance. The silver fitness level requires a bit more experience with exercise, but you still need to hone swimming, cycling, and running skills. You will have a few speed workouts included in your training plans, but you may need more help in two of the three sports. Those in the gold fitness level group have the most exercise experience and more skills. People in this group will still need to focus on improving in one or two of the sports, but they have a basic understanding and background in a low to moderate level of physical activity.

By tallying the answers to all the questions in the TRA, we can begin to assess baseline triathlon fitness and start thinking about the appropriate training plan for your race. Additionally, sport-specific questions in the swimming, biking, and running chapters will help assign you to a proficiency level for each sport. In other words, you might be a gold runner, silver cyclist, and bronze swimmer. We will help you customize a training plan no matter what level of swimmer, cyclist, or runner you are.

Before you start your triathlon experience, it's important to make sure you assess where you are fitness- and experience-wise.

Triathlon Readiness Assessment

Complete the following questions to determine whether you should follow a bronze, silver, or gold training plan as outlined in this book. These questions will help you assess baseline triathlon fitness and guide you through the proper training plans.

1. Classify your current physical activity level:
   a. Not very active (exercise 0–2 hours per week)
   b. Somewhat active (exercise 2–4 hours per week)
   c. Active (exercise 4 or more hours per week)
2. How often do you swim each week?
   a. Never
   b. 1 or 2 days per week
   c. 3 or more days per week
3. How often do you bike each week?
   a. Never
   b. 1 or 2 days per week
   c. 3 or more days per week
4. How often do you run each week?
   a. Never
   b. 1 or 2 days per week
   c. 3 or more days per week
5. How often do you do some form of strength training?
   a. Never
   b. 1 or 2 days per week
   c. 3 or more days per week
6. Do you practice yoga?
   a. No, never
   b. Yes, every once in a while
   c. Yes, one or more times per week
7. Do you do Pilates?
   a. No, never
   b. Yes, every once in a while
   c. Yes, one or more times per week
8. Do you participate in any other sports or activities (basketball, hiking, rowing, and so on)?
   a. No, never
   b. Yes, every once in a while
   c. Yes, one or more times per week

(continued)

9. What is your athletic history?
    a. I never played sports.
    b. I played in high school or college.
    c. I have played after high school or college.
10. How do you evaluate your weight?
    a. Overweight
    b. Slightly overweight
    c. Healthy weight
11. What is your age?
    a. Over 50
    b. 40 to 50
    c. Under 40
12. Do you have any past or current injuries or medical conditions?
    a. Yes, and I am currently under a doctor's care.
    b. Yes, but I have nothing recent or chronic.
    c. No.
13. What is your resting heart rate?*
    a. Over 80 beats per minute
    b. 60 to 80 beats per minute
    c. 40 to 60 beats per minute
14. Do you use heart rate zones?
    a. No.
    b. Yes, but I have never been tested.
    c. Yes. I have had my zones defined by a test.
15. Do you know your lactate threshold?**
    a. No.
    b. Yes. I have been tested and know my LT.
16. Do you know your max heart rate?
    a. No
    b. Yes
17. Do you know how to swim?
    a. No.
    b. I can swim, but I don't know proper technique.
    c. Yes. I know one or more strokes.
18. Do you know how to ride a bike?
    a. No.
    b. Yes, but not very well.
    c. Yes, and I feel confident on my bike.

19. In the past 12 months, what is the longest distance you have swum?
    a. 0 to 250 yards (m)
    b. 250 to 500 yards (m)
    c. 500 or more yards (m)
20. In the past 12 months, what is the longest distance you have biked?
    a. 0 to 5 miles (0 to 8 km)
    b. 5 to 10 miles (8 to 16 km)
    c. 10 or more miles (16 or more km)
21. In the past 12 months, what is the longest distance you have run?
    a. Less than 1 mile (1.6 km)
    b. 1 to 3 miles (1.6 to 4.8 km)
    c. 3 or more miles (4.8 or more km)
22. How many hours per night do you sleep?
    a. Less than 6 hours
    b. 6 to 8 hours
    c. 8 or more hours
23. How many hours per week do you have available for training?
    a. Less than 4 hours
    b. 4 to 8 hours
    c. 8 or more hours
24. What type of equipment do you currently own or have access to? Of the following list, I have
    a. 0 to 4 items available to me
    b. 5 to 8 items available to me
    c. 9 or more items available to me
        ___Swimming pool
        ___Open-water venue
        ___Wetsuit
        ___Stationary bike
        ___Road bike
        ___Triathlon or time-trial bike
        ___Bike trainer
        ___Treadmill
        ___Running trails
        ___Outdoor or indoor track
        ___Free weights
        ___Exercise machine (Bowflex, NordicTrack, elliptical)
        ___Yoga class
        ___Pilates class

(continued)

Triathlon Readiness Assessment *(continued)*

Total your responses as follows:

a = 1 point

b = 2 points

c = 3 points

If you scored 24 through 33, you should start with the bronze program.

As a bronze-level athlete, you are starting from a place where you will have to focus on building a base of fitness and learning proper technique before you start to learn how to go fast and hard. For you, we are going to start by setting the building blocks of fitness. Key factors for you will be establishing a consistent pattern of exercise and eating as healthy as you can to support your new level of fitness. Your pitfalls will come in the form of mental as well as physical fatigue. You will benefit more than those in the other two levels by joining a training group such as a masters swim group, a local bike shop group ride, or a run club. These groups will offer you a method of motivation and support that you will inevitably rely on when you are feeling less than motivated to train. Expect to schedule 5 to 7 hours per week for training.

If you scored 34 through 47, you should start with the silver program.

As a silver-level athlete, you are similar to a sophomore in high school. You know some stuff, but that knowledge will most likely get you into trouble and maybe into detention. We will rely on your beginner knowledge and dive a bit into endurance and possibly some speed. You need to focus on developing your weakest sport while still keeping your strengths sharp. You should begin to explore training outside of groups and find specific training partners who have the same or similar abilities. Expect to schedule 6 to 8 hours per week for training.

If you scored 48 through 60, you should start with the gold program.

As a gold-level athlete, you come into this process with a certain level of skills or physicality. You are most likely quite strong in one of the three sports and will be spending most of your time developing your skill in the other two. You will need to apply your experience in sport to your training. The toughest part of your training will be focusing most of your efforts on your weaker sports and focusing less on your strongest sport. You will be tempted to say to yourself, "I will just make up for it on the run (or bike or swim)," but that approach is wrong. You will have a better experience if you try to have a balanced race, not just a good single leg. Expect to schedule 7 to 9 hours per week for training.

*In general the lower your resting heart rate is, the more physically fit you are. The higher your resting heart rate is, the less physically fit you are. You can determine your resting heart rate by doing the following. First thing in the morning before getting out of bed, grab your watch or phone and use your index and middle finger together to find your pulse either at the radial artery in your wrist or at your carotid artery in your neck. After you find the beat, count how many times it beats in 60 seconds. Or count how many times it beats in 10 seconds and multiply that by six. The average resting heart rate for adults is between 60 and 100 beats per minute. The average resting heart rate for well-trained athletes is between 40 and 60 beats per minute.

**Lactate is the by-product of glucose utilization by muscle cells. Lactate threshold is the exercise intensity at which the blood concentration of lactate or lactic acid begins to increase exponentially. This value is important to note because if the muscles are not trained to clear the lactate that builds up during intense exercise, the buildup can lead to performance issues. The good news is that you can train your body to clear lactate more efficiently.

There are many philosophies about how much time you should invest in training for your event. The key to finding your balance is to define your main limiters and preexisting strengths. Let's start with your third strongest sport, the segment or discipline that you perceive will be the hardest, not only physically but also mentally. Arguably, you should focus the most time and effort on this discipline to develop strength and endurance as well as improve technique. How much time you devote to developing your third strongest sport will depend a bit on what your weakest sport is. For instance, if you are a weak swimmer, you can benefit greatly from spending 3 to 4 hours a week in the water developing your swim stroke technique and endurance. In contrast, if you are a weak runner, spending 3 to 4 hours a week running will most likely lead to injury and frustration. The reason for this discrepancy is that swimming is a zero-impact sport, so your body can acclimate to larger amounts of volume with less risk of injury. Swimming is also similar to speaking a foreign language; the more you do it, the better you get. We will discuss this in detail later in this book.

You must recognize that training for a triathlon is a commitment and an investment in yourself. Making the time to train and following your plan is crucial to your success. Any attempt to cut corners can and most likely will lead to negative results including, but not limited to, injuries and failure to reach your goal. When you follow the program correctly, you will truly understand how satisfying it is when all your training, hard work, good nutrition, and tapering lead to the accomplishment of finishing your first triathlon.

Now that we have established some parameters, you are ready to begin your transformational journey toward becoming a triathlete. Remember this time in your life because after you start this process you will never be quite the same. Gone will be those pretriathlon days; from here on out you will be known to your friends, family, and coworkers as a triathlete! So what do you say, triathlete, should we begin? In the next chapter we'll tell you how to choose a race that fits your schedule and abilities.

CHAPTER 2

CHOOSING YOUR FIRST RACE

Now that you have made the decision to do a triathlon, you need to choose which race that should be. The old saying goes that you get only one chance to make a first impression. The same goes for completing your first triathlon. Because your first race is special and thus extremely important, you want to be sure that it matches your personality and your physicality. In essence, it needs to fit you perfectly.

At first glance you may think that all triathlons are the same. They all require relatively the same things and in the same order, right? Wrong. Dive deeper and you will find that each race has a personality and character that define it. We are going to explore this aspect to help you identify your perfect first triathlon. Remember our gold, silver, and bronze classifications? Those groupings become relevant as we move forward. The key factors we will explore are race distance, race format, topography, proximity, date, friend review or involvement, charitable races, safety, and cost. Each of these factors helps define the personality and fit of the race.

Race Distance

Let's start with race distance. From the beginning of this book we have told you that our focus is training you for a sprint- or standard-distance (Olympic-distance) triathlon. We would like to start by getting one thing straight: Just because you complete a longer event does not mean you are a better triathlete than someone who completes a shorter event. For example, one of the authors, Kris Swarthout, has completed six Ironman triathlons. In comparison, Gwen Jorgenson, two-time U.S. Olympian, Olympic gold medalist, and arguably the most successful professional triathlete, has never completed a race longer than a standard-distance triathlon. Would we ever say that Kris is a better triathlete than Gwen simply because he has completed a longer event? No way. So, for choosing your event we will not imply that because you are choosing a standard-distance race you are better than someone who is choosing a sprint-distance race. Going faster for a shorter period is just as challenging, if not more so, than going longer and not as fast. With that all said, we suggest that our bronze athletes choose a sprint-distance event, our silver athletes choose either a sprint- or standard-distance event, and our gold athletes choose a standard-distance event. Following is a listing of race distances:

- Sprint distance: 750-meter swim, 20-kilometer bike, 5-kilometer run
- Standard distance: 1,500-meter swim, 40-kilometer bike, 10-kilometer run
- ITU long-course distance: 3-kilometer swim, 80-kilometer bike, 20-kilometer run
- Half Ironman distance: 1.9-kilometer swim, 90-kilometer bike, 21.1-kilometer run
- Full Ironman distance: 3.8-kilometer swim, 180-kilometer bike, 42.2 kilometer run

Race Format

Multisport events can occur in various formats. Triathlons are the most common of these, but other formats are also used, including indoor triathlons; winter triathlons of run, bike, ski (Nordic or classic); duathlons consisting of run, bike, run; aquathlons of swim and run; and aquabikes of swim and bike. A nontraditional triathlon can be any combination of the three traditional sports of run, bike, swim. For our training and conversation, we will focus on the traditional format of swim, bike, run.

Another growing style of triathlons is women-only events. For first-time female triathletes, these events can be the best choice for many reasons. First, the event takes the machismo of male athletes out of the equation. Less intimidation occurs from guys who think they know everything and seem to enjoy verbally announcing their presence; you can hear "On your left" only so many times before you feel as if you want to erupt like a volcano. These events are not "powder puff" events. They are well-run, well-organized, women-centered triathlons that cater specifically to women, from training to expo to post party. For all our levels, if you are a woman you should strongly consider these female-only events as your first triathlon. Women-specific triathlons can be found on the event calendar on the USA Triathlon website at www.teamusa.org/usa-triathlon.

Men have the benefit of all the other races in the world being directed to and catered to their traditional desires. Moving forward after your first triathlon, looking toward other formats can offer you great variety based on where you live and what physical limiters you may have. When we speak of physical limiters, we are referencing your third strongest sport and the way in which that leg of a specific triathlon is represented in an individual race. Let's look at a couple examples of how a race may superficially appear to be a reasonable fit but on closer inspection is not the ideal choice for you.

Example 1: Let's assume that you live in a cold northern climate where water temperatures are tolerable only for a short time and you have to swim in a pool for all your training. Let's also assume that swimming is your third strongest sport, but you are working hard to change that. For you, an early season ocean swim event like the historically well run and popular St. Anthony's Triathlon in Florida would not be a great choice. The swim is an ocean swim, and the water can be rough. You can begin to see why this event is not ideal for you. The two major red flags are the swim and the time of year for you as a resident of a northern climate. You should choose a different event as your first triathlon.

Example 2: You are an athlete prone to experiencing running-related injuries such as plantar fasciitis or shin splints. For you, we suggest choosing a nontraditional format such as aquabike (swim and bike only) to keep you engaged. Nothing is worse than training for an event and then being sidetracked with an injury, so why not avoid that issue from the start for your first event? This aspect is one of the hidden gems of the multisport lifestyle. We won't go into training for an aquabike event specifically in this book, but the modifications in the training plan would be simply to swap the run training for swim and bike training accordingly. We would suggest placing 60 to 70 percent of the time toward your weaker sport of the two so that you can develop your technical skills.

Race Topography

For conversation sake, let's assume you have chosen a sprint-distance triathlon. Now we need to spend some time looking at the individual segments or events in that race to see whether they match your abilities. If you are a new swimmer, a race with a traditionally choppy ocean swim, large starting waves, or scary waters may not be the best choice. The swim portion of an event can cause the largest amount of anxiety for new triathletes because of the pure physical contact of the swim start as well as the fact that your face is in the water and breathing occurs only at specific intervals. In the swimming chapter we will further discuss preparation for these factors and ways to overcome the anxiety, but for now, let's not force a square peg into a round hole.

Similarly, if you are a novice biker, choosing a hilly or technically challenging course may not be a good idea. As the old saying goes, "What goes up must come down," and for those who struggle to go uphill with any momentum, you may soon find that the hardest part is on the other side. Descending can bring fear and anxiety. The process of managing speed, braking, and cornering can be a bit overwhelming to newer athletes. If this is the case for you, don't choose a hilly bike course. Many triathlons describe the bike route or even show maps that state the percentage of gradient or angle of steepness. Simply understanding what a 5 percent gradient feels like going up and down can greatly help you define what racecourses best fit you. The best ways to understand a 5 percent gradient is to use an electronic monitor like a GPS, cycle computer, or online mapping tool. You can even find many free applications for your phone that will show you how steep a hill is. If you have none of these things available to you, ask a friend or a local bike shop to point out some hills near you and label the gradient.

Just as a bike course can affect you as a first-time triathlete, the same goes for the running portion of the race. Use the same mapping tools you use to research the bike course to map the run course. During the run you will typically experience the highest heart rates of the event, so understand that even the slightest gradient can radically affect your perceived exertion.

USA Triathlon/Rich Cruse

Make sure you choose a course that topographically fits your skill level.

The most typical way to research all aspects of a triathlon is to go to the event's website. Normally, topographical or elevation maps will be supplied for you to explore. If the event does not supply a useful map option—for example, if all they have is a hand-drawn cartoon—you can cross-reference the racecourse with an online mapping option such as Google Maps. Another option is to check word-of-mouth reviews of the course. Ask your friends and training buddies. Take some time to explore the social media pages of the race to see whether athletes have made any comments about the course. Investing some time in researching the course layout will help ensure that the venue fits you like a glove. At the same time note the timelines of the events. An early-morning start time or late-evening packet pickup time may affect your personal timeline. Race-day preparation really starts a day or a few days before the event at the packet pickup, which is when you collect your race bib number, race swag, and peripheral goodies included in the race.

Race Proximity and Date

Now that you have found a race or several races that fit your abilities, let's see how close to home they are. The first major benefit to choosing a race close to your home is that you have the opportunity to train on the actual event route before race day. Acclimation to the route will benefit you by giving you confidence in knowing the route, which in turn will reduce race-day anxiety. We have mentioned anxiety a few times now, and you should recognize that anxiety is a unique element of heart rate fluctuation that you can control or manipulate by preparation or experience. Think about the first time you drove to someone's house. The original trip may have seemed to last an eternity, but after making the same journey a few times, the drive begins to go by quickly. The same principle applies to training for your triathlon.

The second major benefit is that you do not need to plan extensive travel for your first triathlon. Sleeping in your own bed, eating breakfast in your own kitchen, and making a short drive to the racecourse in your own car on race morning all contribute to lowering your race-morning anxiety. Unknown elements added to your prerace preparations inevitably open you up to the possibility of complications that you do not want or need before your big day. If you do not have any options close to you, look to see whether any friends or relatives live close to a race venue. By not staying in a hotel and not eating restaurant food, you can more easily simulate the benefits of staying at home. If you choose this option, consider bringing a small gift as a means of saying thank you and be sure to invite your friends or relatives to come cheer you on. They will be as excited to see you on the racecourse as you will be competing in the race.

Another large factor is when the race occurs during the calendar year. If you are reading this text in late winter, preparing for a first triathlon in early spring is cutting it a bit close. We suggest a minimum of 12 weeks of preparation for your first event. Reasons for extending this timeline are numerous, but our top three are the following:

- *Allowing yourself more time to gain additional technical proficiency in your third strongest sport.* Becoming a better swimmer, biker, or runner can never hurt. Do not take this to an extreme by postponing the inevitable; you eventually will need to leave the nest of training and do your first race.

- *Calculating for life moments that can pop up unexpectedly and thus delay training schedules or preparedness plans.* When your best friend plans a wedding on your event day, you will be hard pressed not to go to the wedding. The same goes for weather events that can potentially postpone or cancel a race. If something like this happens, you will at least have time to find a replacement event.

- *Factoring in time to research and solve issues that will inevitably arise during your journey.* We hate to mention injuries, but they are not uncommon, and if they occur close to your event, they can quickly shut down the show. Giving yourself some wiggle room is always a good plan.

Whatever your top three personal reasons, the race date must always be factored into your decision-making process. People often place a race on or near an important date in their lives such as a birthday, anniversary, or major life event. These inspirations are all important, but if the date comes at the expense of training, you will be doing yourself more harm than good. A good plan B is to delay the race until next year. We understand that the postponement may seem to last a lifetime, but think about all the good training you can accomplish in the meantime. Whatever the case may be for you, we suggest that after you lock down your first race, you let people close to you know the date. We are not suggesting that you send out a "save the date" card, more just an invitation to come and cheer you on.

Friend Involvement

You will soon discover that although triathlon is an individual sport, unless you are part of a relay team, it is extremely social. You may have a friend who has encouraged you to take on this goal of becoming a triathlete or a friend who is doing his or her first triathlon as well. With either of these scenarios, you now have another element to factor in. Let's assume that your friend has motivated and persuaded you to do your first race with him or her at the friend's favorite race. You now have eliminated a few factors we just discussed, such as race date and location. Sacrificing these factors is OK because you will be participating with your friend. One factor we strongly encourage you not to sacrifice is the race distance. You should still follow our recommendations for the best race distance for you based on your answers to the Triathlon Readiness Assessment. Choosing the right distance for your first triathlon should be priority number one. Your friend should understand and respect this choice; if not, hand the person this book and make her or him read it! Now is not the time to panic if your friend is giving you the high-pressure pitch to register for a standard-distance race when our recommendation is for you to do a sprint-distance race. Many events offer multiple distances for participants on the same day. Check the race website to see whether a sprint-distance race is offered. If not, we suggest sitting down with your friend and discussing this issue before registering for a race.

If you and your friend are both first-time triathletes (or newbies, as we say), then you should both make your race choice based on the factors listed in this chapter. Again, you may need to compromise on a few event decision criteria. If you and your friend live relatively close to each other, we suggest making proximity a priority factor. Race date is a close second on the priority scale. Race distance should have the same personal priority as it did in the previous scenario with your friend who has completed a triathlon before. If you and your newbie friend both score in the same athlete category from the Triathlon Readiness Assessment, you have no worries. If you did not score in the same category but are close, you may need to compromise. If that compromise means that both of you do the longer, or standard-distance, event, you may have a problem. We encourage you to compromise to the shorter of the two events for the benefit of the lower-scoring athlete. If you can't achieve this compromise, we suggest again looking at events that host multiple distances on the same day. Whatever you choose, at least take the time to discuss the factors and how they affect both you and your friend.

Charitable Races

Another factor for choosing a first triathlon is incorporating a charitable aspect to your achievement. Fund-raising for a local school, church, or nonprofit can add an additional level of motivation or accountability to your journey. Many groups, such as Team in Training, specialize in this style of event achievement. They offer race entry, travel accommodations, and group training events. Although these organizations are fine, you're normally pigeon-holed into a small handful of large and traditionally iconic events that will likely require you to fly to a different city. Many of the things we advised you to avoid come into play with these options. Does a singular factor such as raising money for breast cancer research in the name of your mother who recently was diagnosed with stage 3 breast cancer outweigh what we laid out previously? Absolutely not, but we ask you to step back and see the forest for the trees.

We mentioned that these events are normally iconic, so you may ask, "What makes these events iconic?" Good question. The answer is that iconic events include epic and unique race segments. The Escape From Alcatraz triathlon in San Francisco has you swim from Alcatraz Island to shore, which is not the best option for a new swimmer. The water is cold and choppy and contains a strong current, and you start the race by jumping off a boat. We will not even get into the whole shark aspect of this swim. You begin to understand what we mean by iconic. The New York City Triathlon has you swim in the East River, again probably not the best option for our bronze group or anyone just learning to swim. Think about where Tony Soprano and his friends dump bodies, weapons, and evidence. The current alone can be enough to frighten even the most seasoned swimmer. For some, these iconic elements become the reason they do the race—to overcome the seemingly impossible.

USA Triathlon/Rich Cruse

Choosing a charitable race can make the experience even more enjoyable.

We advise you to hold off and save these for your triathlons in the coming years. We suggest you get one or two races under your belt before you tackle them. This way, you will not come into them completely green and will be able to absorb the true beauty and wonder that always come from doing an iconic race. Other ancillary issues we would like you to avoid in your first triathlon are issues like packing and unpacking your bike, dealing with airline travel with a bike, or trying to complete your race on a rented bike in an unfamiliar town. Why take on any of these extra stressors during your first triathlon if you don't need to?

Race Safety

You should also consider the safety of the triathlon and the venue you have selected. Many factors contribute to a properly run and safe event. Some well-known races and race directors have been around for a long time, and some events are new. To make a good choice for your first race, talk to your friends and relatives or send an e-mail to USA Triathlon for feedback on the event you are considering. You'll want to see whether the race has been USAT sanctioned; check the USA Triathlon website (www.usatriathlon.org) and use the key word "events" to help steer you to the current list of national sanctioned races. You should be able to see whether the race you want to do is listed there. The benefits of participating in a sanctioned event include, but are not limited to, the fact that athletes want a worry-free race experience; they want to show up on race day and be able to focus on their own race with minimal distractions. USAT-sanctioned events provide that positive experience because these reasons:

- benefit from the collective wisdom of over 35,000 sanctioned races completed over the last 30 years;
- deliver athlete peace of mind by ensuring that industry-wide safety standards are observed;
- ensure a fair race governed under industry-standard competitive rules;
- provide the gold standard of insurance protection for the event, athlete, and venue;
- provide ranking points for regional and national rankings, including annual designations of USA Triathlon All-American status;
- exclusively provide the opportunity to qualify for national championships and then qualify for world championships as a member of Team USA;

- post results for all events; and
- support the national governing body and enable it to develop new programming, grow the sport, and fund initiatives including youth participation, the Olympic program, and paratriathlon. USA Triathlon's mission is "to grow and inspire the triathlon community"—a virtuous cycle that directly benefits each race director and all athletes at all sanctioned events.

Some of the safety areas that are addressed at a USAT-sanctioned event include water quality, air temperature at race start, water temperature the day before and day of the race, the number of kayaks or canoes that will be in the water during the swim, the number of athletes per wave of the swim start, the number of aid stations on the bike and run routes, the number of USAT-certified officials on the race-course, the number of doctors and nurses on site in the medical tent, and monitoring of weather considerations (storms, lighting, rain, hail) that might require modifying race distances. This list is not all inclusive, but it gives you a good idea of all the safety considerations that a race director must meet to sanction a race with USAT. When a race is sanctioned, the race director is held accountable for the highest standards to remain in compliance.

If you are considering a nonsanctioned race, ask yourself these questions:

How high are the safety standards?

Some race directors may want to cut corners on safety by avoiding USA Triathlon's stringent sanctioning criteria (usually to reduce costs).

Is the race organization solvent?

Is the organization strapped for cash? Is there a flight risk? Unfortunately, in a few cases race directors have taken participants' money and folded without any accountability.

What is an event hiding by not sanctioning?

The fact that a race director is unwilling to share information with the national governing body is often a red flag for numerous underlying issues.

Does the event offer participant accident coverage?

Some race directors insure only themselves from liability. USA Triathlon provides coverage to race directors, athletes, and volunteers in all its sanctioned events.

Is the organization following industry-accepted rules?

Is the organization using industry-trained officials? Events sanctioned by USA Triathlon operate strictly by the rules, and officials at sanctioned events are expertly trained to enforce the rules fairly and safely.

Is the water properly tested for contaminants?

You have no assurances that the water is tested in nonsanctioned races.

Would you trust a doctor without a medical license?

If not, why would you risk participating in a race that has not been sanctioned? Sanctioned events are produced by certified professionals who have been trained to a standard deemed acceptable by the national governing body. When a sanctioned race says it is safe, you can feel confident that it is because USA Triathlon has reviewed it and approved it.

We strongly encourage you to choose a USAT-sanctioned race for your first event. We want your experience to be positive, fun, and safe.

Race Costs

Finally, you'll want to consider the cost of registering for your first triathlon. A local sprint-distance race is your best bet for a lower-cost experience, although traveling to an event is often part of the excitement. If you are lucky enough to find a sprint-distance or standard-distance race in your hometown, then you have to pay only for the cost of race registration, assuming you have already purchased your swim gear, bike gear, and running gear. A quick online search finds a sprint-distance race in California that costs $85 to register; this compares with a standard-distance race in New Jersey that costs $135 to register.

If you plan to drive to a race, consider the cost of staying in the host hotel, which is usually the one closest to the race venue and is in proximity to restaurants. Renting a condo with a kitchen might be a lower-cost alternative that allows you to prepare your own food the days before and morning of the race, which can help you avoid any unwanted GI distress. Or perhaps you have friends or family who live near the race venue and will let you stay with them, thus allowing you to save money. If you fly to an event, you'll need to consider how you will transport your bike. Airlines charge up to $150 each way to fly with your bike, in addition to the cost of your plane ticket, and sometimes they don't handle bikes with care. Another option is to ship your bike from a local bike shop to a bike shop in the event city. You will pay a small fee for the home bike shop to tear down the bike and another fee for the second shop to reassemble the bike at the race venue.

Now you are ready to kick back, fire up your favorite online machine, and explore the Internet to find your triathlon. Closely research your choices. Remember that you get only one shot at your first triathlon. We want that first time to be memorable for positive reasons, not negative issues that could have been prevented with a few simple clicks of the keyboard. After you have narrowed down your race choices or chosen your event, ask a person who has done triathlons what they think of your selection. Such feedback can be a good bit of reassurance that you have chosen wisely, or the person may be able to provide information that may not be commonly found online. If you don't know anyone, another resource is a local triathlon or bike shop. People there should be more than happy to give you input or feedback. Happy hunting and choose wisely. Our next stop will be choosing your gear.

CHAPTER 3

GEARING UP

Triathlon over the past few years has become extremely gear centered. Every couple of weeks some new and improved gadget or gizmo seems to come on the market. This onslaught is enough to leave even the best of us spinning and wondering what is actually worth investing in. The basic tools of our sport are a suit and goggles, a bike and bike helmet, and a pair of running shoes. This collection seems simple enough, but we are going to take an in-depth look at what you should invest in now and what you should save up for to buy later.

Swimming Gear

Having the right gear for swimming is important. Some gear is considered communal property in some pools, whereas in others there is nothing to be found. For this purpose we want to run down the needs, wants, and must-haves for swimming, starting with the basics.

SWIM BAG

The first thing we need to look at is your swim bag. Because going to the pool is itself often an event, we suggest that you have a specific pool bag setup that will always accompany you. Several types of bags are on the market: mesh, duffle, and backpack. We have even seen shopping-style bags on the deck. A good swimming bag should allow ample airflow to assist in the drying process after your workout and should contain a separate wet or dry pouch or area. We mention the shopping bag only because we have seen a few plastic shopping bags used as pool bags in the past and have cringed when we examined and discussed the issue of mold growth in pool equipment. Proper storage, cleaning, and drying of swimming equipment will ensure that your gear lasts as long as possible, stays in good working shape, and doesn't get you sick along the way.

SUIT

Inside your bag should be a few staples and a handful of optional items to make each swim workout enjoyable. For the men, the choice of suit can often send shivers down your back. The mere thought of putting on a set of briefs can prevent many of you from ever hitting the pool deck. Breathe easy and know that there is another option for you out there, called jammers. Jammers are a skin tight, non-lined style suit that extends down to the mid-thigh or to the top of your knee. Jammers look similar to triathlon shorts but do not contain a pad and are normally lower in price. A typical brief is less expensive than a jammer. Both options can be found at your local swim supply store or online. They should be tight but should not limit movement. Over time, the chemicals from an average pool will cause wear and tear on your suit. You need to care for it by wringing it out in cold water after each workout. A light detergent can be used if needed, but simply tossing your suit in the wash with your other linens is not recommended. For women, a standard one-piece suit is typically the norm in the pool. Many women's suits offer both a longer leg cut as well as a brief style cut on the bottom. The same care practices apply to women's suits.

GOGGLES

Equally as important as a suit in your swim bag is your goggles. Goggle technology has come a long way in the past 10 years, but the same essential rules apply. Your goggles have to fit and be watertight. When shopping for goggles, try on numerous pairs to find the one that best fits your head and eyes. Note here that while swimming you should not cry because the same silicon barrier that keeps pool water out also keeps your tears in.

We group goggles here into three categories: standard, mask, and minimalist.

Standard Goggle

Starting with the standard goggle (see figure 3.1), you need to be aware of a few fit points to ensure that you have a comfortable and sealed line of sight. The contact point where the skin around your eye meets the actual goggle is your first concern. Normally, a standard goggle has some sort of soft silicon seal that creates the watertight barrier. The second fit point to look at with goggles is the spacing arch or bridge that goes over your nose and between the two goggle lenses. Some basic goggles supply multiple pieces that snap into this area to allow self-adjustment, whereas other models have fixed bridges and offer different sizes of goggles to accommodate this gap. Either way, the goggles must fit your particular eye spacing and remain comfortable. A common mistake that swimmers make is to smash their goggles to the face to make a tight, waterproof seal. This level of security is vital only to swimmers who dive off starting blocks as part of their routine. Swimmers who only push off from the wall do not need to have their goggles strapped down this tight. Goggles that fit properly seal with a moderate level of strap tightness. The final

FIGURE 3.1 Standard goggles.

variable in your standard goggle selection process is the tint or finish on the lens. If you are swimming indoors in a pool, a standard clear lens will suffice. If you swim outside, we suggest purchasing a clear or yellow tinted pair of goggles for overcast days and a pair of smoked or mirrored goggles for sunny days. Having these two pairs will be beneficial when it comes to race day, but we will explain that in a later chapter. If you wear glasses, you can buy prescription models that will enable you to see better and not have to switch to contact lenses.

Mask Goggle

The second style of goggle you should look at is a mask-style goggle. This type of mask goggle is not the same kind that you go snorkeling with in the Bahamas; it does not have a nose cover and is substantially less bulky. When shopping for a mask-style goggle, all the same principles used to fit a standard goggle apply. One fitting trick for mask-style goggles is to push them into your face, force out excess air, and see whether they stay suctioned to your face. If they do, you have found a good fit; if they don't, keep shopping. Remember that when trying on masks, your hair can corrupt the seal, so make sure to pull it back before trying them on. Masks can offer swimmers a greater range of vision, which can come in handy on race day when sighting swim buoys. Let your personal preference take precedence when choosing a mask or standard goggle.

Minimalist Goggle

The third style of goggle is the minimalist goggle, sometimes referred to as the socket rocket. These simplistic goggles have little or no silicone sealant around the contact area. They have a simple string bridging the nose, and the strap normally consists of a basic piece of elastic band. Many old-school swimmers use these goggles because of their relatively cheap price point, but be aware that they normally have the smallest field of vision, are not available in prescription, and can be uncomfortable. Whichever style of goggle you choose, buy a couple of pairs because they always seem to break at the most inopportune time.

WETSUITS

Another piece of swim equipment you need to consider is a triathlon-specific wetsuit (see figure 3.2). These are not your common scuba wetsuits; they are skin tight, super flexible, and extremely slick on the exterior. A properly fit wetsuit can help you by taking anywhere from 5 to 7 seconds off your time for 100 yards (m). It is made of multiple thicknesses of neoprene and acts like a giant life jacket. A wetsuit gives you a high level of buoyancy, which will improve your body position in the water and ultimately helps you swim faster by reducing hydrodynamic drag.

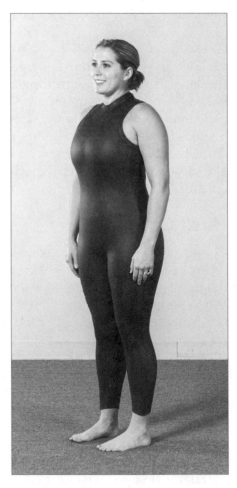

FIGURE 3.2 Triathlon-specific wetsuit.

Wetsuits come in two main styles: sleeveless and full sleeves. Some people find the sleeveless style more comfortable because it offers less resistance in the shoulders, thus creating less stress in those muscle groups. Traditionally, the more you spend, the better fit you will obtain. If you find a midrange suit that fits you well and you experience no discomfort with it, we suggest you stick with that. A note about shopping for wetsuits: You will quickly find that they are cumbersome to put on, so you may be tempted to get one that is slightly oversized. But remember that the wetsuit should fit skintight and restrict your breathing just a little. A good triathlon store employee should be able to help you with sizing. After you find your size, buy some body lubricant to help you get your suit on and off during practice and races. You will want to apply the lubricant to your calves, ankles, and neck area. If you have trouble getting the suit over your ankles, we suggest trimming the suit up at the bottom of the legs a few inches (5 to 10 cm). You won't damage the suit, and by creating a larger opening, you will be able to get the suit off faster when it counts.

You should know that not all races allow the use of wetsuits. Water temperature is measured by the lead official or race director the morning of the event. The results of that measurement guides whether wetsuits will be allowed. According to USAT rules, if the water temperature is 78 degrees Fahrenheit (25.6 degrees Celsius) or below, then wetsuits are allowed. At 78.1 to 83.9 degrees Fahrenheit (25.6 to 28.8 degrees Celsius), participants may wear a wetsuit at their discretion, but wearing a wetsuit in that temperature range will mean that the athlete is ineligible for awards. At 84 degrees Fahrenheit (28.9 degrees Celsius) and above, wetsuits are not permitted; this rule is for the athletes' safety. Before you arrive at the race site, you may hear some preliminary notification about water temperature. Pay attention to the official notifications being communicated before and on race day and know that the official water temperature will not be announced until race morning. We suggest you always bring your wetsuit just in case.

OPTIONAL SWIM EQUIPMENT

Optional equipment includes fins, a pull buoy, a kickboard, and a snorkel. Swim fins are not the standard scuba fins; they have a short lip that normally extends 1 to 3 inches (2.5 to 7.5 cm) out from the tip of your toes. These fins are used to help account for lack of propulsion during certain swim drills. They also come in handy during longer kick sets. Be careful in how much you use them in the beginning. Like any new tool, your body must acclimate to their use. Your calves will thank you later.

A pull buoy (see figure 3.3*a*) is a piece of buoyant foam or rubber that is placed between the legs, just below the crotch. It helps you by providing additional flotation during drills, and you can use it during pull sets when you are swimming only with your arms and not using your legs to kick.

Kickboards (see figure 3.3*b*) are pieces of foam about 18 inches (45 cm) long, 10 inches (2 cm) wide, and 1 to 2 inches (2.5 to 5 cm) thick. A kickboard is used to help during kick sets. You normally rest your arms on top and wrap your fingers over the front lip. Many pools have these on deck, so you may not need to get your own.

The last thing is a snorkel (see figure 3.3*c*). Again, the snorkel is not the traditional scuba snorkel that runs along the side of your face; this

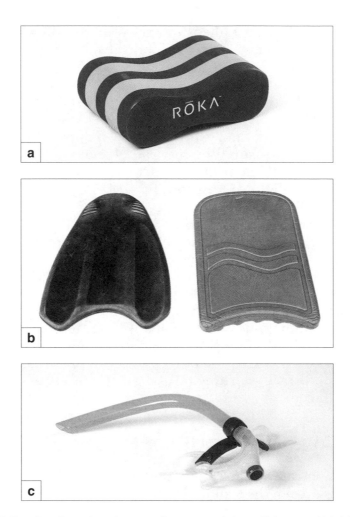

FIGURE 3.3 Optional swim equipment: (*a*) pull buoy, (*b*) kickboard, and (*c*) snorkel.

snorkel wraps up the front of your face and has a strap that goes around the forehead area for support. Snorkels can be helpful in working on balanced and even strokes. Using a snorkel helps you develop a smooth stroke by eliminating the need for you to roll to the side to breathe, which may be causing timing or rotation balance issues.

Finally, you should always have some shampoo and soap in your bag for showering after your workout. Chlorine can do serious damage to your skin by drying it out. Washing properly after your workout and applying a small amount of lotion can prevent you from aching all day after your swim workout.

Biking Gear

Of the three sports in triathlon, nothing compares with biking in terms of potential cost and sheer nerd value. Biking has a rich tradition that many triathletes seek to adopt. We will break down the needs from the wants and toss in a few must-haves.

BIKE

The expensive part of triathlon is the bike. You have a few options when looking at bikes. Do you need a fancy triathlon-specific bike to do your race? The answer is no. Honestly, any bike that fits you reasonably well will do. We have seen people race with everything from BMX bikes to single-speed hipster bikes.

Let's assume you need to get a bike for your first race. Your best bet for a first bike is a road bike, not a triathlon-specific bike. The main reason is that you need to learn to drive the station wagon before you can take out the Ferrari. Learning to ride, handle corners, and ride near other athletes is best done on a road bike. A road bike can be purchased for as little as $750, but if you look more into the $1,300 range, you will find higher quality components and frame. This small investment will pay off when you begin to service your bike. When shopping for a bike, set your budget and take that number with you to the bike store. When setting your budget, remember that you will need to spend an additional $100 to $300 on necessary add-ons that normally do not come with your bike.

PEDALS

Most new bikes do not come equipped with pedals. We suggest that you invest in clipless pedals (see figure 3.4a) that allow you to attach your cycling shoe to the pedal temporarily, much as a ski boot attaches to a downhill snow ski. These pedals create a semilocked connection between a bike shoe and the pedal itself. Clipless pedals are safer than the traditional toe clips that are found on platform pedals (see figure 3.4b) because in the event of a crash, your shoes will come unclipped automatically, much as ski bindings do, and not trap your foot. If your foot is trapped, the chance of breaking a bone in your leg or ankle increases significantly. Another benefit is that the clipless pedal allows you to pull up on the pedal during the pedal stroke, allowing you to create more torque, leading to more speed.

Kris Swarthout

FIGURE 3.4 Pedal types: (*a*) clipless pedals are recommended because they are safer than (*b*) platform pedals, which aren't as common today.

The other half of the clipless pedal equation is the shoe. Unlike a mountain bike or spin class shoe that has treads on the bottom for walking around, a standard road bike shoe has a smooth bottom. A characteristic of all bike shoes is a solid, nonflexible sole. This stiff sole will help ease the stress on your arches as you bike increasingly longer distances. Triathlon-specific shoes tend to have only one or two straps to help ease the process of getting into and out of the shoes quickly. Triathlon shoes are not necessary for your first race, but they may be an item to consider buying the next time you get bike shoes. At a base level, you can use platform pedals, or basic pedals that have no mechanism to connect the shoe to the pedal. These pedals allow you to bike in your running shoes, but they limit the amount of power you can generate on the bike. For your first race this type of pedal is acceptable, but we encourage you to transition quickly into using clipless pedals to limit stress to the foot and increase your power generation on the bike. More about shoes is coming up!

HELMETS AND ACCESSORIES

Safety equipment is a highly recommended purchase for your bike. A helmet is a must. Gone are the days of bikers wearing tiny Euro hats with flowing hair. Invest in a well-fitting helmet that matches your bike color and looks good on your head. If you are going to skimp on a purchase, this is not the place to do it. Known as brain buckets, melon caps, and coconut protectors, helmets all have one purpose—to protect your brain in the case of a crash. Lowballing this purchase is short sighted. One thing to keep in mind when choosing a helmet is that the more holes it has, the more airflow it supplies and the cooler it will be. On the other hand, the more holes it has, the less protection it offers. Look for a happy medium in this area.

After choosing your helmet, look at purchasing some flashing lights for the front and rear. If you plan to ride on the open roads during training, you definitely want to be seen. You will not need lights during your race, but they are worth the money to keep you safe when training. Sunglasses are another useful accessory that will help keep road grit and bugs out of your eyes and the sun at bay.

SHOES AND CLOTHING

When choosing bike shoes, start with a well-fitting shoe. As with any shoe, comfort is most important. Cycling shoes differ from normal shoes because they have a stiff, or rigid, sole. This feature allows you to experience less fatigue in your arches and apply consistent power to the pedals.

You will find that cycling shoes come in variety of styles, colors, and formats. Mountain bike shoes normally have a deep tread on the bottom that makes them good for walking in. Likewise, spin bike or gym bike shoes are easy to walk around in. Road-cycling shoes normally have a smooth bottom with little or no tread. They typically have small raised bars near the toe and heel to protect the bottoms as you walk, but be careful because these shoes can be slippery in wet conditions. The third type of shoe is a triathlon-specific cycling shoe (see figure 3.5). These shoes normally have

FIGURE 3.5 Triathlon-specific shoes.

a lower heel cup, fewer straps, and sometimes no tongue. They are designed so that you can get them on and off quickly. Choose shoes that are appropriate for you and your ability, but most of all make sure they are comfortable.

Cycling clothes, like cycling shoes, are designed for different types of biking. Mountain biking clothes normally fit looser. They resemble normal clothes but have thigh-fitting liners. Traditional cycling clothes are tighter fitting and are often referred to as spandex. The reasons for the tight-fitting designs are mainly to eliminate chafing and to decrease wind drag. Baggy clothes are more likely to cause chafing in places you don't want, and baggy clothes that flap in the wind lead to slower riding speeds.

We recommend making the investment into a good cycling kit, which includes a pair of bib-style shorts and a jersey. Bib shorts have a chamois in the crotch that acts as a bit of padding for your comfort. Note that this chamois should be in contact with bare skin to achieve optimal comfort. Bib shorts also have straps that rise and go over your shoulders. This design gives better coverage against the elements around your waist area. The jersey should have two or three pockets in the back for storing your keys, phone, or food. On longer rides you can put gloves or other items in there too. A good jersey should fit snugly but does not need to be skintight.

Cycling clothing offers you an opportunity to display your love of your sport or define your athletic spirit. We have seen many things on cycling clothes from beer ads to rainbow cats with lasers coming out of their eyes. Loud, bright colors are acceptable in cycling clothes because they help drivers, pedestrians, and other bikers see you. Match your kit with a comfortable pair of athletic socks and maybe a cycling hat if you want to dress to the nines.

FLAT TIRE NECESSITIES

Odds are that at some point you will experience a flat tire. Therefore, we suggest that you have a saddlebag containing a few vital elements. You need to carry two bike tubes, because one is never enough. You'll also need a set of tire levers to help you remove your tire from the rim and a small pump or CO_2 cartridge inflation system. If you choose the CO_2 system, practice using the cartridges before riding. They are a one-shot deal, and figuring out how to use them when you are far from home is not a good plan. Before you ride, take a moment to wrap some duct tape around the cartridges before you pack them in your bag. When you open them, the compressed air causes the cartridges to

TRAINING INDOORS

For those days when life gets crazy, the weather doesn't cooperate, or you just don't want to go outside, you have a few options. If you belong to a gym or cycling studio, you can do a class on a spin bike. This activity is better than doing nothing, but beware of relying on these classes too much as your training progresses. Many spin bikes have fixed positive drivetrains, which means that they don't coast. This action is fine for spin class settings, but it doesn't exactly simulate the outdoors. Another concern with classes is that they normally include a large amount of extra movement that you would never do when riding. The bottom line is that classes are good for burning calories but not so good for training for your race.

We prefer bike trainers that connect to your bike and provide resistance to the rear wheel. Such trainers allow you to ride your own bike in your choice of locations—basement, garage, or in front of the TV. These types of trainers come in one of three main styles: wind resistance, magnetic resistance, and fluid resistance. Normally, wind resistance units are the least expensive, but they are quite loud. Magnetic resistance units are a bit more expensive and offer only a limited amount of resistance based on the magnets used by the trainer. Fluid trainers are normally the most expensive, but they are traditionally the quietest units, and they provide gradual resistance change based on speed. Whatever trainer you choose, you should have a fan, a towel, and a water bottle nearby during your training sessions. Some manufacturers recommend purchasing a specific trainer tire for use with trainers, but we don't find that necessary. The main thing is to ensure that your rear tire is pumped up to 120 pounds per square inch (8.3 bar) each time you ride. Doing this will ensure a longer life span through lower friction.

When completing bike workouts on a trainer, remember that your training time needs to be modified. When you move from the road to the trainer, you lose a few key factors—coasting downhill and stopping at stop signs. Both of these actions give your workout a little break and allow you to catch your breath. The rule of thumb is that 45 minutes on the trainer equals 60 minutes on the road. We have written all the workouts in this book as if you were going to be riding outside on the road, so if you move things indoors, make this mathematical adjustment.

freeze. If your fingers have any moisture on them, they will stick to the cartridge like that kid's tongue stuck to the pole in *A Christmas Story*. You will thank us for this tip later.

OPTIONAL ADD-ONS

A few optional add-ons you may look to invest in later are aero bottles, an aero helmet, race wheels, and aero bars. But notice that if an equipment name starts with the word *aero*, it is not necessary for your first race. These items are usually made of carbon fiber and may cost more than your bike. If you plan to start upgrading, look at upgrading your whole bike because some of these items come standard on more aggressive, higher-end bikes.

Finally, a bike computer is a valuable tool that will tell you how much time and distance you have put into your workout. A basic computer should have speed, time, distance, and RPMs. You can spend more to get more information, but to start, this is enough. Bike computers come in both wired and wireless options. We think that the wireless option is worth the money. As a maintenance item, you should plan to change the batteries in the computer head and receiver module at least once a season.

Many phone applications now offer data tracking similar to what bike computers provide. If you choose to use this option, look for a secure mounting system that allows your phone to be displayed relatively close to your line of sight. Be aware that if you choose this option, when you crash (trust us, it will happen sooner or later), your phone will likely take the brunt of the force. A crash could destroy or severely damage the unit.

Running Gear

The cheapest discipline in our sport is running. Shoes, shorts, and a shirt are really all you need, but as we have shown so far, you have many additional options to consider. In addition, there are always gadgets and gizmos you can add to enhance the experience.

SHOES

All you really need for running is a pair of good-fitting running shoes. We recommend shopping at a running store and getting fit by a professional. Expect to be asked to walk or run on a treadmill, which is part of the process of finding the right shoe for you. Some words of advice here: Purchase your running shoes in a half size larger than your normal street shoes. Your foot tends to expand and flatten out over the duration of your run, so a larger show will help prevent black or dead toenails. Be sure that the toe box is wide enough for you. Not all shoes are designed the same way. If you have wide feet, get a shoe that accommodates your foot shape. Lastly, invest in a pair of elastic shoelaces. These laces function as a time-saving mechanism when you go from the bike to the run. They also allow your foot to swell during your run. Elastic laces are cheap and will ensure that your shoes never come untied again during a run.

CLOTHING

A typical triathlete trains and races in a triathlon suit. A tri suit can come in either one piece or two. The suit is normally form fitting and made of a material similar to spandex. Normally, you wear the tri suit during the entire race. A tri suit should be cared for as if it were a delicate piece of clothing. To help it last longer, wash it only in cold water with a mild detergent. A good pair of athletic socks helps ensure foot comfort during the bike and run, and a bike jersey is a good item to wear during bike training.

RUNNING ACCESSORIES

One thing you should never overlook is a good-quality sunscreen. With your increased time in the sun, you will be exposing your skin to the elements. Preventing sunburn and eventually skin cancer is in your best interest. One last little piece of equipment worth purchasing is a number belt. This strap of elastic normally has two clasps. You wear it around your waist and attach your race number bib to it. The belt prevents you from having to pin your number to your jersey, and you can put it on after you exit the swim during your first transition.

Finally, after you have acquired all your gear, look at purchasing a triathlon bag. This larger backpack-style bag can hold all your equipment as you walk from your car to the race. It functions as triathlon luggage when traveling from place to place when training, traveling, or racing. Many brands and styles are on the market, but a good one will have a compartment for your wet clothes. Keeping these separate from your dry clothes before or after a race is a luxury you can afford. As with the swim bag discussed earlier in this chapter, be sure to air it out well after each use and clean it periodically.

Now that you have all your equipment, let's explore who you are going to take with you on your triathlon journey. We'll discuss your triathlon support group next.

CHAPTER 4

YOUR TRIATHLON SUPPORT GROUP

One of the keys to your success in training for and completing your first triathlon, besides putting in all the training time, is your support group. Your journey will be much easier if you find people who want to help you complete your first triathlon by offering moral support, providing childcare support, motivating you, being a workout buddy, or just cheering you along the way. These people can include your significant other, friends, family, kids, babysitters, coach, training groups, triathlon clubs, coworkers, online bloggers, and anyone else you enlist to help you successfully complete this journey.

Training Groups

Groups can be beneficial for the newer athlete. They can offer motivation, knowledge, and a fun sense of community. Many types of group training opportunities are available in the sport of triathlon, a direct benefit of being made up of three sports. We will touch on the major types of group training and address what you should look for when scoping them out.

SWIMMING GROUPS

Depending on where you live and pool availability, you may have several options to join a swimming group in your area.

Where to Look

Regardless of your swimming ability, you should consider joining a swimming group. If you belong to the YMCA or another health club that has a lap pool, then that resource is valuable for you because the club may offer coached group swims either in the morning, at lunch, or in the evening. Some colleges and universities offer swimming programs that the public can pay to join. Depending on your location, you may have the option of joining U.S. Masters Swimming, which provides coached swim workouts (for a membership fee) for its members several days per week.

Don't let the name fool you; *masters* refers to age, not ability. The workouts usually have a theme for each day; one day may focus on skills, another day on speed, and another day on endurance. The lanes are usually set up so that swimmers of similar skill swim together. Beginners normally swim in the first few lanes, and the more advanced swimmers work in other lanes. The workouts are a good way for new swimmers to learn how to circle swim and begin to understand the etiquette of swimming in a lane. Many masters swim groups offer introductory swim instruction for beginner swimmers. You can check out the offerings available in your area by visiting the USMS website at www.usms.org.

If you are a younger athlete looking for a pool that has a swimming club, team, or group to swim with, the YMCA, community pool, or local colleges may offer swimming programs that you can join.

Or, if you are lucky enough to live near clean, open water, groups likely meet to do open-water swims. These groups are a bit different from masters groups. You will likely not have a structured workout, but a coach or leader may give some instruction in the beginning. Open-water swims with groups are beneficial because they allow you to acclimate to the challenges of nonpool swimming within the safety of a group. Look for local triathlons to organize these groups or single swimming events. You can also search your local parks and recreation websites to

Joining a masters swim group can help you meet new training and racing partners.

see whether any local governmental units are hosting events at beaches in your area. These training groups give you excellent opportunities to find new triathlon training friends and support as you move forward.

What to Ask

When you do find swimming groups or clubs in your area, be sure to ask a few key questions including the following:

How much does it cost to join the group?

Normally, a swimming group must charge a membership fee for access to the pool. Pools with lap swim are in high demand, so facilities charge groups to rent lanes. The group then passes those fees on to its members. Most charge a monthly fee, which gives you access to swim with the group 3 or 4 days per week. Depending on where you live and whether the group has a coach (a coached group will cost more to cover the coach's fees), you are probably going to pay between $45 and $75 per month.

What is the schedule for practicing—early mornings, lunchtime, and so on?

You want to ask when the group swim practices are scheduled and find a group that practices when you can be there. For example, if the group swims three mornings per week from 5:30 to 7:00 a.m. and then on Saturdays from 6:00 to 7:30 a.m., but you can't make early morning swims, you'll need to look elsewhere. Some groups offer early morning, lunchtime, or evening swims, or a combination of all three.

Does a qualified coach lead the swim workouts?

Not all groups are led by coaches certified by USA Triathlon or USA Swimming. Check to see whether the swim sessions are coached or whether the group is just a swim-as-you-like group. Most groups offer a prescribed workout for the day; for example, Monday is drill day, Wednesday is endurance day, and Friday is sprint day. Not all will prescribe a daily workout, so you can use the swim workouts we prescribe later in this book.

What level of swimmers are part of the group?

Many swim groups include all level of swimmers, ranging from bronze to gold. In most cases, lanes are designated for the bronze swimmers, silver swimmers, and gold swimmers based on how fast participants can swim 100 meters. This way, swimmers of similar ability are grouped into lanes so that the flow of the lane works well for everybody.

Are fins, paddles, and kickboards supplied?

If you want to use any equipment while swimming, such as fins, paddles, or a kickboard, you will likely need to buy those items. Some groups, however, offer as part of their membership fees access to a limited amount of swim equipment that is stored at the pool and is available on a first-come, first-serve basis. Check with your swim group to see what is available.

What are the benefits for members? Besides access to a swimming pool, does membership offer any other benefits?

These benefits could include discounts on swimming gear and apparel, coach-led workouts, and possibly access to other features that the swimming facility offers, such as a gym.

CYCLING GROUPS

Whether you are a bronze-level athlete or a gold-level cyclist, you can benefit from joining a local cycling group, workout or ride, or club. A cycling group can provide motivation to ride, safety in numbers while on the road, a planned route or workout, a group of like-minded people, and the opportunity to learn and practice key cycling skills.

Where to Look

Bike shops are a great source of information to find out whether any local ride groups meet in your area. Such groups organize weekday and weekend rides based on experience level and sometimes gender. For a beginner female athlete, not having to mix it up with a bunch of men can be comforting. Look for women-specific or newcomer-specific groups or clubs in your area. Likewise, if you are a silver-level athlete who is looking to be pushed just a bit, a stronger group of riders can help further your fitness and bike-handling skills. You'll want to inquire with the organizer about the skill level of the riders in the group. You may want to ask around to confirm that the "Sunday coffee ride" is not secretly a "Sunday sufferfest."

Many group rides turn into a sufferfest—a ride that is extremely aggressive and challenges even the best cyclists. Some sufferfest rides even have professional cyclists join them on occasion just to keep things interesting. If your plan isn't to go hard and fast that day, you might want to reconsider joining a sufferfest. Some of the most enjoyable rides are what cyclists call coffee rides. These rides are perfect for lower-energy days and recovery days. Traditionally, the pace is relaxed, conversation is abundant within the group, and the destination is a favorite coffee shop with wonderful pastries. These types of rides have a rich European tradition, and they continue today in America. For a coffee shop ride, pack a few dollars and a few stories to share; you will learn to enjoy these rides as much as you do the sufferfest rides going forward.

What to Ask

When you do find cycling groups or clubs in your area, be sure to ask a few key questions including the following:

Is the ride a "no drop" ride or a "no wait" ride?

On "no drop" rides, the entire group stops if someone has a problem. The group may stop at certain points to ensure that the stragglers catch up and everyone finishes together. This kind of ride is beneficial for less-experienced riders because the stress and expectation of each athlete is lower. "No wait" rides, on the other hand, do exactly the opposite. These rides tend to be extremely aggressive. If you have a problem or start to fall back, it is on you to catch up or find your way back.

How far does the ride go?

Group rides usually have two distance options—anywhere from 15 to 20 miles (25 to 30 km) for beginner riders and 25 to 30 miles (40 to 50 km) for more advanced riders. Normally, the group establishes an agreed-upon turnaround points for those who are riding the shorter distance, or the group may ride one or two loops of a designated route depending on whether they are doing the shorter or longer distance.

How many people normally show up?

Knowing how many people traditionally show up to a ride is important because large groups can be intimidating to newer, less-skilled riders.

How hilly is the ride?

This characteristic depends on where you are riding. In Colorado Springs, we have hills, mountains, and more hills, but someplace like Kansas may be flatter. You'll have to ask the group ride leader about this before you go to the first group ride.

Do most riders use road bikes or tri bikes?

In some pure cycling groups, triathlon bikes are either not allowed or discouraged because triathlon bikes are not normally the bike of choice when riding in tight pace lines or drafting groups. The aero position that riders assume does not allow quick emergency braking, and the aerobars are seen as spears to riders in front of you.

What is the average pace?

Knowing the group's average pace can help you determine whether the group is riding at your level before you get in the sticky situation of either having to try to hold on to the back end or yawning at the front. Average pace can be deceiving. When in doubt, start with a slower group and move your way up.

Does the ride break into subgroups, one with a faster pace and one with a slower pace?

On most group rides, a faster group heads out and does a longer distance as described earlier and a slower-paced group does a shorter distance. Regardless of your pace, you should be able to find other riders with a similar pace in the group. A beginner cyclist should avoid doing her or his first group ride with a pro-level cycling group because the action will be intimidating.

What are the benefits for a member?

Not all cycling groups have formal membership. People may simply meet informally on Saturday mornings for a group ride. But a cycling group with membership fees might include benefits such as discounts at the local bike shop, discounts at upcoming races, and possibly a special member party after a local race.

RUNNING CLUBS

If you want some running motivation and are looking for other people to run with, a local running club is a good option. Normally, groups include a mix of pure runners and triathletes, so you'll fit right in. Some running clubs do early morning workouts, whereas others meet in the evenings.

Where to Look

As with the relationship between bike shops and bike groups, run stores can be a good first place to find a run group. Most run groups are training for a specific event like a marathon or 10K. Pick the group that best suits your first goal distance. For example, you would not want to join a marathon training group if your first race involves only a 5K run. If you are fortunate enough to have a triathlon store nearby, you may be able to find groups that do bike and run brick sessions.

These workouts would be ideal for your training, whatever your level.

Most running clubs hold a group run 1 to 3 days per week. All levels and abilities are usually welcome, and two routes are normally offered— a longer one for those looking for a workout of up to 6 miles (10 km) and a shorter one for those looking to run about 3 miles (5 km). Runs are normally segmented during the week to one of three basic formats— recovery, speed, or distance— and they are usually placed during the week in that order. Start with a less aggressive pace group to see whether the pace is truly what the group says it is. As with biking, the egos inside a group can quickly turn an advertised easy run

Find a group to run with that best matches your training goals.

into a fast-paced collegiate cross country race in no time. Again, assess these groups on the Internet and find out what others are saying about them. A great resource for running clubs in your area is the Road Runners Club of America (www.rrca.org). In addition, most fitness clubs have some sort of run club. If you belong to a club, check to see what is going on inside your club; it is another way to maximize your dues.

What to Ask

When you do find running groups or clubs in your area, be sure to ask a few key questions including the following:

Does the running group charge a fee to join?

Not all clubs charge a fee; many are informal gatherings for like-minded people to get together and run.

How often are group runs scheduled?

Find out what the group schedule is. For example, does the group offer runs one night per week, or do they get together two mornings per week and every Saturday? As mentioned earlier, find a group that runs when you can make it so that it works in your training and life schedule.

What kinds of runners attend?

Running groups offer a social aspect that many people really enjoy, and many groups cater to a wide range of running abilities. Some of the group go out fast and run 6 miles (10 km) or more, and others are a bit slower and run 3 or 4 miles (5 to 7 km). The beauty of this kind of group is that you can always find someone of similar running ability to run with.

What are the routes?

The running group likely has a normal route for each run. This arrangement could vary based on how often the group meets, but you can expect a shorter run route of 3 miles (5 km) and a longer run route of 5 to 6 miles (8 to 10 km). The route may be and out and back with a designated turnaround place, or it could be a loop route with one loop for the shorter-distance runners and two loops for the longer-distance runners.

Do people run in pairs, small groups, or as one large group?

Running groups normally end up dividing up into smaller groups and even pairs as the faster runners go out front and the slower runners fall behind. The group may naturally split up into smaller groups as people of similar running pace run together.

What are the benefits for a member?

The benefits of joining a running group might include group runs, discounts at a local running store on running shoes and gear, discounts for entry into local running races, possibly a coach who leads the workouts, and the social aspect of running with people like you.

TRIATHLON CLUBS

A triathlon club is the holy grail of training groups. Instead of trying to be a multisport athlete fitting into a single-sport club, you will be surrounded by like-minded athletes every time.

Where to Look

One of the best resources for finding a triathlon club near you is the USA Triathlon website (usatriathlon.org/findaclub). By joining a club sanctioned by USA Triathlon, you are guaranteed to get the resource that best fits your training with the benefit of available guidance from trained professionals and leaders in our sport. A good triathlon club will have not only group training sessions but also social events and group races in which the majority of the group's members train and race together. These events offer a safe and rewarding atmosphere for you before, during, and after the race.

A club often has a unique club uniform that will help you identify others and help others identify you during a race. This connection will come in handy when you are feeling fatigued and ready to slow down. Normally, just at that moment a fellow club member will spot you and give you that little bit of encouragement that will help you finish strong.

USAT clubs can be found all across the country and can connect you with like-minded people for training, racing, and fun. Members of USAT clubs also enjoy special benefits including discounts at some club races, a club challenge competition, a club newsletter, and much more. Many clubs offer group training sessions and educational seminars. To find a USAT club near you, search by using the keyword "clubs" at www.usatriathlon.org. You should find all the information you need there. To maximize your contribution to the sport that is fueling your lifestyle, become an annual member of USAT and receive even more benefits and opportunities. You won't regret it.

What to Ask

When you do find triathlon-specific groups or clubs in your area be sure to ask a few key questions including the following:

How much does it cost to join the club?

Clubs have different entry fees based on their activities and ancillary add-ons like uniforms or swag. Know what you are paying for on the front end. If they don't tell you, simply ask.

Is the club USAT certified?

USAT-certified clubs offer benefits like insurance, team competitions, entry into regional club championship events, and season competitions. All these features separate USAT clubs from simple unaffiliated local clubs.

Is the coach USAT certified?

USAT coaches have a base level of knowledge and are insured by the organization. CPR training, SafeSport training, and criminal background checks are all part of the annual USAT certifications, but these items may not be required for a non-USAT-certified coach.

How often do they meet to swim, bike, and run?

Knowing that the group meets enough to meet your needs is a basic requirement. If you join a group assuming that it meets every day and then it doesn't meet at all, you will be disappointed to say the least. Do your research.

Where do they meet to swim, bike, and run?

Find out whether a group's activities are located close to you and whether participation requires an additional fee. If groups meet daily but you have no access to the activities because they take place far away or you lack the funds, you will be disappointed.

Nontraditional Support

Some days you may not be motivated to get out of bed early to go swim, bike, or run. Or you may not feel like going to the gym after work to get your workout in. For those reasons, having a support system to encourage and push you will be helpful. When you share your triathlon goals with other people, they can help you hold yourself accountable to get the training done. Also, by talking about your goals, you are leading by example and showing your family, friends, coworkers, and kids the importance of pursuing a healthy lifestyle.

YOUR FAMILY

Ideally, your family is supportive of your triathlon journey. If you are worried about how to fit in the swimming, cycling, and running workouts with everything else you have going on, don't worry. By making the commitment to train for a triathlon, you are setting a healthy example for your family. You can make workouts fun by including your spouse or significant other. For example, you can do a Saturday morning run together and then get coffee and run errands. If you have kids, you can include them as well. Riding bikes together as a family or having a child who is old enough ride his or her bike alongside you while you run is a healthy family activity. If you are lucky enough to have grandparents nearby who are willing to watch your kids while you do a longer weekend workout, take them up on the offer when your training plan calls for it. If you swim at the YMCA or other local pool and can swim with your kids, you have another good opportunity to spend time together and get your workout in.

You need to be willing to compromise; on some days you may have to get up very early before everyone else in your house to get the training in and then spend the rest of the day doing family activities. You may also consider your day off from training to be the day you are the busiest with activities; it will be one less thing to try to get done. Some people choose races based on their destinations so that they can take the whole family and turn the event into a vacation or long weekend. Be flexible and realistic; ideally, your support system will be there to cheer you on during the race. When your race is over, be sure to pay back your family for all their support by spending some time doing something they want to do. Maybe you can take the kids to a movie and get an ice cream and take your spouse or partner out for a nice dinner. They are more likely to support you in the future for another race.

YOUR FRIENDS

If you have signed up to do your first triathlon with a friend, that friend might be just the training partner you need. For some people, knowing that another person is waiting on them at 5:30 a.m. for an early morning swim, bike, or run is just the motivation they need to get out of bed and go. Friends can also be supportive of your healthier lifestyle. You may be able to shift some of the activities you do together to include taking a yoga class, going for a hike, taking a healthy cooking class, or going to the gym together.

Take time to share your goals and aspirations with your friends and let them do the same with you. By linking your goals together, you begin to create a stronger bond and your training will begin to line up with more synchronicity. Be sure to avoid the pitfall of always defaulting to one person's workouts. Remember that a friendship is like any other relationship; it's based on trust, equality, and communication. By incorporating your friends and family in events and workouts, you begin to grow in the sport and in your life. Triathlon will soon introduce you to people you may never have had the opportunity or inclination to meet. This opportunity to expand your circle of friends is a gift that few other sports offer. Never close off your doors; always look to others for inspiration and embrace the differences you find in each other. Ultimately, you will grow more as a person than you would have ever thought possible before you began your journey toward completing your first triathlon.

YOUR COWORKERS

Most of us spend at least 40 hours each week working with other people. This large block of time that we spend with our bosses and coworkers is

ONLINE BLOGS AND INFORMATIONAL WEBSITES

You may occasionally need to obtain some triathlon training support from the comfort of your keyboard. If you are looking to read inspirational stories, study race reports, and chat with other people who are training for their first triathlons, you might consider reading online blogs for beginner triathletes. USA Triathlon offers several blogs from a variety of writers that can be found at www.usatriathlon.org. Use the key word "blogs" to be directed to a fair amount of pertinent content. Be aware, however, that the online world will expose even more hidden pitfalls than you find in other parts of the sport. If you have a question about an issue, asking it in a blog or forum can open up a can of worms. Many people want to show you how much they know by simply telling you what they think. People may start a statement by quantifying their status by saying, "I have been doing triathlons since . . ." or "I have done 14 Ironmans so . . ." or even "I have won five triathlons, and I think . . ." These people may mean well, but in the end they are creating more noise than content. Our suggestion is to read content from a variety of sources, find the common messages and information, discuss it with your closest training buddies or coach, and then go out and train. Don't be sucked in by trolls whose only goal is to get your goat.

a good place to find support for your triathlon goals. If you have a few work friends who are also interested in training and racing, enlist their support to help keep you motivated and accountable for getting your workouts done. If you are lucky enough to work in a building that offers an on-site gym or gym access, take advantage of it! Schedule yourself a 30- or 60-minute break (schedule and boss permitting) and do a quick run, strength workout, or bike ride. Maximize your available break by packing food so that you can eat right after you finish or at your desk. Have a bag of gear and some extra clothes at your work space in case you forget or a spontaneous work buddy workout is proposed. Do you work with someone who also likes to swim, bike, or run? If so, do a buddy workout once a week with that person.

But let us offer a word of advice: Be careful about how you go about living your dreams at work. Some people out there will not see things the same way you do, and they may take issue with your newly found motivation. Try to be subtle with your accomplishments and accolades. Don't leave your tri bike in your cube with all your gear hanging off it.

Yes, you are proud of your sport, but others may get a bit tired of constantly being reminded about it, especially if they are struggling with their own fitness goals. Be sure not to air out your sweaty clothes on your chair and desk; one whiff of body odor from an old shirt can turn everyone against you in the drop of a hat. In short, play it cool, be subtle, and know which work friends you can brag and boast to. They will be your trusted inner circle during the workday.

In addition, be cautious as a triathlon newbie; you are like a young zebra surrounded by hungry lions. Many people will want to give you advice, sell you their products, and get you into their gear. You must choose your support group wisely so that you can vet a number of these new opportunities with them before pulling the trigger. You will likely begin to receive advice from multiple people and sources. This counsel can be confusing because it will likely be contradictory. One person might say, "Get a tri bike, now!" whereas another source might say, "A tri bike can wait; you really should start with a road bike." The key is to find people you trust and listen to them. Otherwise, you will be trying to drink from a firehose.

The more people you can engage with and share your triathlon goals with, the more motivation and support you will have during the hard days of training and the exciting days of racing.

Now that we have formulated a plan to create your support group or entourage behind you for your first triathlon, let's start with the real training. Our first stop will be the swim. Prepare to get wet.

PART II

IMPROVING YOUR TRIATHLON TECHNIQUE

CHAPTER 5

SWIMMING

The first discipline in the traditional triathlon is the swim. For the purpose of this book we assume that you have a basic level of competency in the water—that you can get from one end of the pool to the other without stopping. Our goal in this chapter is to teach you the basic phases of a swim stroke so that you can identify where you need the most improvement. By understanding your weaknesses, you can better focus your training to improve in those areas.

Refining Your Swim Stroke

Because swimming is a technical sport, simple improvement in one area can have residual benefits in others. For instance, by simply improving an issue such as eye and neck position, you can improve your body position and level in the water.

Each of the five main phases of a swim stroke plays an essential part in the execution of a complete stroke. Just as the backstroke and weight transfer in golf play an intricate part in how far and straight you hit the ball, the arm recovery and hand entry are important to the proper overall execution of a swim stroke. Let's take a closer look at the proper execution of each of these phases.

ENTRY

The entry, as shown in figure 5.1, is the point where the hand enters the water fingers first and palm down. The entry point should be about halfway between the tip of your nose and the point where your hand fully extends away from the body. The hand should enter the water cleanly and create a minimal amount of bubbles as it extends forward to its furthest most extension point. This hand travel path should be flat and in line with both the body line and the surface of the water. The fingertips should end about 4 inches (10 cm) under the surface of the water.

FIGURE 5.1 Entry.

During the entry, your eyes should remain focused toward the bottom of the pool and your neck should remain in a neutral position, meaning that it is in line with the rest of your spine. This neck and eye position should remain constant throughout the entire swim stroke cycle except when you breathe.

Some of the common errors seen during the entry are improper hand position in which the thumb enters the water first, hand entry too far forward causing the arm to slap in the water, and eyes rising to look forward. By allowing the thumb to enter first, you introduce another element of motion into the stroke because you will have to roll the hand to position it for the catch. This angled entry can also contribute to a slight deviation in your course that may not be evident in the pool but will often materialize in open-water swimming.

Practice the hand entry in shallow water by standing and slowly going through the motion. Have a partner watch to see whether you are doing what you think you are doing. Repeat this movement multiple times at different paces to ensure that you can execute it during your normal stroke. Slapping your arm in the water not only creates unwanted resistance by allowing your upper arm to enter first but also causes more drag by not entering at the most efficient angle. This result is visually evident by the production of bubbles. Your eyes should always be looking toward the bottom of the pool at about an 85-degree angle from the level surface of the water. When you look forward you take your neck out of neutral position and cause your hips to drop. A simple exercise to establish this is to stand straight and then look up. You will notice that your hips eventually roll forward and your neck begins to hurt (see figure 5.2a). Instead, keep your eyes down and your neck neutral (see figure 5.2b). If you're afraid of the wall, use your peripheral vision and trust that the tee at the end of the black line will

FIGURE 5.2 Establishing a neutral neck position: (a) incorrect and (b) correct.

never move and will always be the same distance from the wall, every lap. A great way to promote keeping your eyes down is to swim with a snorkel. The simple breathing position required to avoid sucking water into the snorkel will show you the correct head position.

CATCH

The catch, as shown in figure 5.3, is the point where you first begin to grab water. The arm stays straight forward, but the wrist bends to a 90-degree angle, leaving the fingers pointing toward the bottom of the pool. The catch is a simple yet often overlooked element of the swim stroke. Most swimmers move from the entry straight to the pull because they fail to see the importance of the catch. This small motion anchors the hand in the water and sets up the pull. The catch phase is your first chance to grab water and create forward velocity.

A mistake often seen is a lack of any catch at the beginning of the stroke. A good exercise to help promote the catch and strengthen your forearms is sculling. Sculling is simply cupping the hands in an

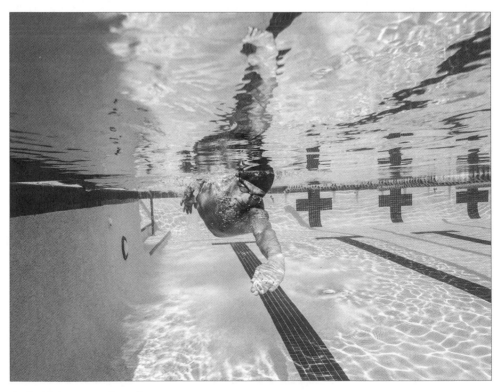

FIGURE 5.3 Catch.

attempt to catch water without any other movement of the arms (see figure 5.4). With your arms stretched in front of you, slightly cup your hands and bend your wrists so that your fingers point toward the bottom of the pool. You should kick slightly but not so much that you negate the purpose of the drill, which is to create forward velocity with your hands. The kick should be just enough to keep your body horizontal in the water. Move your arms in quick, horizontal movements to maintain your head above the water's surface. Think of scooping out a big bowl of brownies with your hands or think of your hands as canoe paddles that you are moving left and right to pull your canoe into a dock.

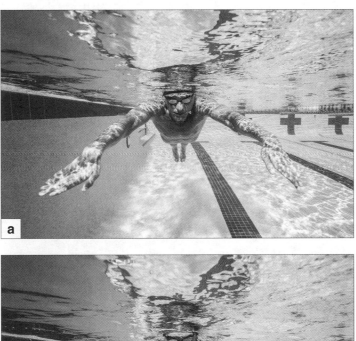

FIGURE 5.4 In sculling, both hands work symmetrically to create pull by cupping water and moving back and forth. Notice the minimal bend in the elbows during this drill.

PULL

The pull, as shown in figure 5.5, is arguably the largest producer of velocity in the entire stroke. The pull begins with the engagement of an early vertical forearm. Essentially, after the wrist bends, the next joint to be engaged is the elbow. As the elbow bends to 90 degrees, the fingers remain pointed to the bottom of the pool and the forearm moves to a vertical position, creating a large pull surface with the inside of the forearm. The forearm vertical position should occur before the hand travels past the shoulder. After vertical position is achieved, the hand and forearm should travel back along the body towards the hip. This path should remain straight and within 8 inches (20 cm) of the body. The straight travel path maximizes forward velocity by creating direct thrust backward. By keeping the hand and forearm close but not too close to the body, you maximize the use of leverage. For the same reason, you don't carry a large box far away from your body because you are not strong in that position; you can move more water faster if your hand and arm are closer to your body. Avoid getting too close because you will then be

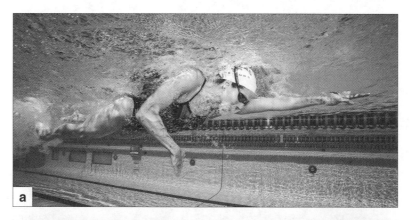

FIGURE 5.5 Pull.

pushing water that is already flowing around your body. At that point you lose power because the water you are pushing is already going backward.

A common mistake seen during the pull is a lack of early vertical forearm, or EVF. Instead, swimmers round the hand and arm down, pushing most of the water to the bottom of the pool. The hand and arm stay flat in the water and contribute little or nothing to forward thrust and velocity. A great exercise to promote early vertical forearm is the fist drill, which is as simple as it sounds. Instead of using your palms to grab water, you swim with a closed fist, forcing the forearm to catch and move the majority of the water during the stroke. As you do this, you should feel the water affecting the inside skin of the forearm. You should also feel a bit more tension in your shoulder. To understand this, stand on dry land, stretch your arm out in front of you with your elbow facing up, and keep your hand extended with your palm facing down (see figure 5.6). If you do this correctly, you should feel a tightening in your shoulder area; we call this an engaged shoulder. Only when the shoulder is engaged will you be able to execute correct early vertical forearm position. Athletes commonly drop the elbow as the shoulder fatigues, thus losing the ability to execute early vertical forearm positioning.

FIGURE 5.6 (*a*) Shoulder is not engaged. (*b*) Shoulder is engaged, which will lead to proper forearm position during the pull.

EXIT

The exit, as shown in figure 5.7, is the phase of the stroke when the hand finishes the pull and leaves the water in route to the recovery. The exit may seem insignificant, and if done properly, it should have little to no effect on the stroke. But if the exit is done incorrectly, it can cause an imbalance in the following phases. During the exit, the hand should push and exit the water past the hip with the fingers still pointed toward the bottom of the pool. The hand should not twist or flick as it exits the water.

The two most common mistakes in the exit phase are an early exit and improper hand position as it leaves the water. An early exit normally occurs when you attempt to swim fast. The goal is to increase your stroke count to achieve greater speed, but what often ends up happening is that you shorten your stroke, which decreases the velocity you create. Ultimately, you end up doing what looks like a dog paddle—fast strokes with little speed. You are better off keeping a forceful long stroke than having a fast turnover. If your hand is not in the correct position and it leaves the water (fingers down), you will likely end up pushing water to the surface, not behind you. This action not only diminishes your forward velocity but also pushes your body down slightly. This slight movement can then affect body position, which in turn increases drag. You begin to see how one thing can affect numerous other phases down the line.

FIGURE 5.7   Exit.

RECOVERY

The recovery, as shown in figure 5.8, is the time when you give your hand a short rest. During the recovery, the elbow should be high in the air to promote good body roll, and the hand should dangle limply with the fingers just above the water. The path should be straight forward from the exit point to the entry point.

A common error often seen during the recovery is winging or flailing the arms out to the side. Winging or flailing is caused by inadequate body roll. When the body doesn't roll to an angle of 35 degrees or greater, the shoulder does not allow the elbow to bend and recover in a high position. A flat body position forces the hand to recover wide. This action may not affect you in the pool, except when you whack your lane mate in the head as he or she passes you going the other way, but in open water your arms will not be able to recover over waves and you may smack other swimmers over and over again in a packed triathlon swim group.

One of our favorite drills to correct this issue is a fingertip drag drill with zipper. As your hand leaves the water, drag your thumb up the side of your ribcage like a zipper while at the same time dragging your fingertips across the water. This body position forces you to roll and ultimately helps you recover in the correct position.

FIGURE 5.8 A high elbow and relaxed hand are easy ways to spot a proper recovery.

Training for the Swim

We are now going to address numerous aspects of swim training and focus on how you as a beginner can progress from simply swimming back and forth in the pool with no purpose to doing effective training in the pool and then taking the skills you have learned in the pool out into open water.

POOL TRAINING

For several reasons, most of your training will occur in a pool. Pools provide a safe and controlled environment for swimmers of all abilities. Pools are consistent. They never get longer or shorter, their temperature is normally consistent, and the clarity is usually the same. Pools give you a structured environment in which you can accurately measure improvement, intervals, and overall distance. Indoor pools are the only way that many people can swim all year round. For those reasons, all levels of swimmers do most of their training in a pool because they benefit from its features.

Note that if you are timid in your swimming skills, you should never swim alone or without a lifeguard present. Even if you are a proficient swimmer, things outside your control can happen. If someone else is in the pool or watching you, she or he can save your life when you can't save your own.

Individual Pool Training

If you train alone, always come to the pool with a plan. Don't just jump in the pool and do some laps. You will never make real progress if you are not swimming a workout. A workout should have a defined warm-up, drill set, main set, and cool-down. Many swim workouts can be

---

SWIM WARM-UP

Before you start any swim training in the pool or open water, you should warm up your muscles a bit. If you have access to stretch cords, you can do some simple exercises on the pool deck before jumping into the water. A few simple warm-up exercises that you can do with stretch cords are alternating one-arm rows, alternating pull-ups, two-arm rows, and biceps curls. If you don't have access to stretch cords, you can jump in the water and swim an easy 100 to 150 meters before beginning your workout.

found on the Internet and in the training programs listed in this book. Swimming is an extremely technical sport, meaning that it requires the athlete to be technically proficient, not just strong. You can't muscle your way through the water; you need to move through it by maximizing leverage propulsion and repeated movement.

Practicing swim technique over and over is the only way to get better, just as you must practice a foreign language to improve. We believe that swimming two times a week for an average of 60 minutes per workout is the minimum that an athlete can do to maintain swim form. By moving to three or four times a week, the swimmer begins to improve technique through frequency and muscle memory. As you are swimming, you must be thinking about your stroke at all times, doing internal diagnostics while you swim. If you can identify whether you completed a stroke correctly or incorrectly every time, you will begin to improve a little each workout. To this end, we do not encourage the use of swim radios because these gadgets distract you from focusing on your stroke.

Group Pool Training

Many pools and gyms have adult swim groups who train together. These groups are commonly referred to as masters swim groups. The word *master* refers to a person's age, not his or her skill level. Benefits of masters swimming are comradery, guidance, and structure. Getting up at 5 a.m. in the dark and cold to hit the pool can be difficult on the best days, but if you have friends who will hold your feet to fire if you don't show, that can often be all the motivation you need not to skip the workout and sleep in. Most masters groups have a swim coach on deck who designs the workouts and watches you from the deck. This coach can give you feedback on your stroke and help you refine your technique. Workouts are often structured with progression during the season and become slightly more difficult over time.

A national group called U.S. Masters Swimming holds swim meets for adults and offers insurance and continued education for athletes and coaches alike. Some groups ask their swimmers to be members of this organization as part of their membership dues. For athletes who travel and wish to swim when on the road, U.S. Masters Swimming can assist in finding swim groups in towns around the country. If you are a beginner swimmer, masters groups can be a great way to locate a swim coach who can assist you in your training.

Another resource for stroke development is Total Immersion. The TI model is a popular method of learning to swim, especially for older swimmers. The development of movement and technique is taught through a series of lessons that normally helps the athlete become a proficient swimmer. More information can be found by visiting www.totalimmersion.net.

TRAVELING AND SWIMMING

If you are a businessperson who travels regularly, you may need to establish a plan B when your only option is a small hotel pool or no pool at all. In this situation a little planning can go a long way. Let's start with attempting to locate a pool or masters group for you. Simply go to your favorite Internet search engine and type in "open swimming [destination city]." The result should provide you with a few options for pools near where you will be. A second search could be for a nearby masters group. U.S. Masters Swimming has a useful website, www.sms.org, and from their home page you can search for registered groups in any area of the country.

If you don't want to swim masters and the only pool is a small hotel pool that would not be conducive to lap swimming, you can build a simple swim tether (see figure 5.9) that allows you to swim in place. All you need are an old bike tube and a 5-foot (150 cm) piece of stretch band. Take one-third of the length of bike tube and create a loop by tying the ends together. This loop goes around your ankles. Take

FIGURE 5.9 A simple homemade swim tether can turn any pool into a training pool.

the stretch cord and tie it to the bike tire loop you just made. Now pair that with a swim buoy and a snorkel, and you are set. You put the bike tube loop around your ankles, tie the stretch cord to a fixed object like a pool ladder, place the spin buoy between your legs, and mount your snorkel. You will be able to swim in place using just your arms, no kicking needed. Place a few pennies on the bottom of the pool to give you a frame of reference about where you are and then vary your stroke speed to allow you to swim in front of or behind the pennies. You can swim other strokes with this setup and not lose fitness on the road. To practice kicking, simply turn and kick against the pool wall. This system is not perfect, but it will get you to your next workout, and it is better than nothing.

If no water can be found, use a set of stretch bands to simulate your swim stroke. Wrap the band around a fixed object like a pole, bend forward to make your torso horizontal (sitting on a fitness ball works well here too), and simply practice your stroke technique. You can do sets of 20 strokes as your fitness allows. You can also use these bands to warm up in the morning before you race if the event does not allow you to get into the water before you start.

OPEN-WATER TRAINING

After you have become comfortable with swimming in the pool, when you can confidently complete a 30- to 60-minute workout, you are ready to take your skills to the open water.

Swimming Close to Shore

Many people have a misperception that open-water swimming needs to be done from one point in the water to another a long ways away. But we encourage you to start close to shore and swim parallel to the shore. You only need to be in waist-deep water, and most swim beaches work just fine for this. You can swim using the swim buoys for sighting and boundaries. That way, you'll be safe and can practice in a comfortable area. If you choose to venture out deeper and farther, never do this alone. Always bring a partner and tell someone where you are going and when you will be back. The vast majority of deaths in triathlon occur during the swim. Don't put yourself at any great risk when you don't have to.

Sighting

When you begin to swim in the open water you will soon notice the lack of a solid black line under you. One of the most common mistakes athletes make in open water is going off course. By simply swimming in a straight line you will be one of the better swimmers in your race. Swimming straight requires balanced and equal swim strokes from your right and left arms. Think of a tank or bulldozer; it needs both tracks to travel at the same speed to go straight. The same goes for your swim stroke. All your time in the pool is now going to pay off. You will begin to see that technique outweighs strength as you move from point A to point B in the open water. Sighting on fixed items in your path or on the horizon will also help you swim straight.

Sighting is the simple act of looking up during your stroke to confirm your position and heading. You should sight every five to seven strokes in a consistent pattern. Sighting too often causes excess shoulder and neck strain and can lead to slowing caused by inefficient body position. By not sighting often enough, you risk going way off course and making the swim much longer than it needs to be. If you are a right-side breather, the sight comes as you extend your left arm forward during the entry. Exhale, lift your head up so that your eyes exit the water, and look down at your fingers. Look quickly, because you have only a fraction of a second. Inhale and round the head to the right, allowing it to reenter as if you were breathing to the side normally. Practice this movement while standing in shallow water and not moving forward before you try to incorporate it into your stroke.

Overcoming Anxiety

Many people are concerned about swimming in the open water. If this is the case, we suggest a few things to make it easier on yourself:

- Always swim with a partner. A person swimming with you is safer than swimming alone.
- Establish a mantra: "Just keep swimming" seems to do the trick. Reciting a mantra over and over can help the mind focus on something other than what is below you.
- Focus on your breathing. You will not only feel your breath but also hear and see it. Focus on the pattern, the bubbles, and the sound of your breath. Make a song out of it and think about blowing bubbles in the tub. This simple act of distraction can allow the mind to focus and assist in reducing the anxiety of open-water swimming.

In addition, some participants fear the feel of the weeds or other plant life. If this is the case for you, we suggest that you wear a wetsuit. But remember that not all races allow wetsuits, and in other races, water temperature guidelines determine whether they are allowed (see the section on wetsuits in chapter 3 for more information).

Preparing for the Race

Now that you have practiced in the pool and then taken those skills to the open water, you are ready to line up for your race.

CHOOSING A SWIM START

For your first race, no matter what your skill level, we recommend choosing a race with a beach start, meaning that you will start out of the water and run in to begin. Some races have you start in the water, and you begin by treading water. As you progress in your triathlon career, you will also likely experience the three main race starting styles—mass start, wave start, and time-trial start. Each of these three main starting styles can be done either at the edge of the water or in deep water. The most important thing to know is what you will see on your race day. If the race does not state the starting style on its website, check race photos or ask other athletes who have done the race before. Here is more information about the three starting styles:

- *Mass start.* All competitors start at the same time. Many races are going away from mass starts for safety reasons, but if you should find yourself lined up for a mass start and you don't feel confident in your swim, we suggest lining up near the back. When the gun goes off, wait a second, let the masses rush in first, walk into the water, and start at your own pace. This approach eliminates much of the washing machine effect, but you should know going in that you will be kicked or punched at some point, so be ready.

- *Wave start*. Athletes are grouped into starting waves of anywhere from 50 people to just a handful. A wave normally comprises people of the same gender and age. Sometimes it is made up of athletes with similar skills and abilities. The same rules apply here. If you feel skittish, simply line up toward the rear and enter slowly.
- *Time-trial start*. The athletes enter the water one at a time or in pairs at a prescribed interval, normally 2 seconds. This style of swim start is normally the safest and causes the least amount of athlete-to-athlete contact and anxiety.

ORIENTATING YOURSELF

As you are standing on the shore waiting for your swim to start, you should concentrate on the swim buoys in the water. Note their color, how many there are, the first one you will turn at, and the shape of the buoys. The perspective from the water during the swim can be quite different. A helpful method is to sight on a secondary landmark that is on the horizon or shoreline beyond the buoy. A boathouse, big house, or distinctive tree can be a good backup when you have trouble seeing the buoy. Make sure that the item you choose stands out sufficiently. If it blends into the background, it will be useless to you during the race. The last thing you should do before the gun goes off is to wipe a little spit inside your goggle lenses and then rinse them out. This trick will help prevent fogging in most goggles. When the gun goes off, begin swimming toward the first swim buoy, remembering all your technique tools.

OVERCOMING CHALLENGES IN THE WATER

Should you find yourself in a spot of bother at any time, simply stop, raise your hand, and wave it toward a swim safety person or lifeguard. You can hold onto a raft or board while you gather your composure and then move forward to resume the race. Race personnel cannot help you move forward, but they can legally offer you a rest.

As you approach the turn buoy, stay to the outside of it and don't get involved in the thrashing that commonly occurs next to the buoy itself. Swim around it and continue to the next one. As you round the last buoy, look for the swim exit, which is normally marked with flags, an arch, balloons, or some other marker. Sight on it and know that you are near the end of the swim.

EXITING THE WATER

As you approach the beach begin to think about the steps you will be taking as soon as you stand up. Begin to think through the checklist of steps you will take in transition 1 (T1). In addition, begin to ready yourself for the feeling of lightheadedness that can come when you first exit the water. Your body has been in a horizontal position for some time, and moving it to a vertical position will cause a shift in your blood pressure, sometimes leading to slight dizziness. If you know that this feeling is coming, you can anticipate it and ready yourself to fight through it. Now, as you near the shore, you should swim until your hand touches the bottom. At this point you should stand up and exit the water. Pull your goggles onto your forehead and breathe deeply; you're one-third of the way done with your first triathlon!

Historically, the swim portion of the race causes the most anxiety in athletes, so for some the race is over before they even begin. This apprehension doesn't need to affect you. By taking the proper steps in training and mentally preparing yourself for what is to come after the horn sounds, you are sure to have a better swim than most. Remember to stay calm, swim straight, and think positively. Before you know it, you will be back on land and heading out on the bike.

Now it's time to move into T1, where you need to get out of your wetsuit and into your cycling gear. As you approach the transition area, begin to think about the steps you will be taking to remove your swim-specific equipment. The first thing is to get to your transition spot as quickly as possible (taking the time to remember where you racked is important!). When you get to your rack, take off your gear and lay it on the ground. Put on your helmet, socks, and bike shoes if you have them, put on your glasses, grab your bike, and head to the bike-out gate. Look for where everyone else is going if you are a bit lost. Be sure to run your bike in transition; you are not allowed to ride inside the transition zone. Cross the mount line and begin your next journey, the bike.

CHAPTER 6

CYCLING

Cycling is traditionally the second portion of a race. It is the longest distance of the race, and it requires the most equipment of all the sports. We have already discussed most of the cycling gear you need in chapter 3, so the focus of this chapter is on cycling safety, skills, etiquette, and training. So grab your bike, helmet, and cycling shoes, and let's get riding!

Cycling Safety Awareness

Before you head out on the road to ride your bike, let's make sure you have everything you need to do so safely. Before every ride you should conduct a simple list of safety checks to ensure a safe, productive training ride. Your bike safety checklist should include the following items.

BIKE

Before you ride, start by looking at the bike as a whole, giving it a visual once over before you focus specifically on designated areas. You may want to clean any dirty parts at this time. A simple glass cleaner can be used safely on most surfaces to remove dirt and bugs. We will talk about the greasy parts in just a bit.

Brakes

If we had to choose the most important working part of your bike, it would be the brakes. If your brakes don't work properly, your day is going to go sideways quickly. The best way to approach them is taking it step by step, as follows:

- Squeeze the brake levers (see figure 6.1a) to ensure that the cables are in good, working order. The brake handles should travel or squeeze the same distance in each hand. The cables should squeeze and release with ease and should not bind at any point.
- Look to see whether the brake calipers near the tires (see figure 6.1b) have functional movement, meaning that they open and close smoothly as you squeeze the brake levers.

- Give the wheels a spin to ensure that the brakes are not rubbing on the braking surfaces of the wheel rim. If rubbing occurs because your wheel rim is wobbly or out of true, we suggest you take your bike into your local bike shop for a tune-up. If only one pad is rubbing, you can usually move the brake caliper around so that is centered on the rim and not rubbing. If you can't keep the brake from rubbing, have your local bike shop fix this issue.

- Squeeze the brakes and push the bike forward to ensure that the brakes have the power to slow and stop you when required.

FIGURE 6.1   Brake components: (*a*) levers (*b*) calipers,

Headset

The headset is the area where the fork and the stem, which holds the handlebars, come together (see figure 6.2). Headsets come in several designs based on your bike and its specific components. Basically, the headset is a set of bearings that allows friction-free movement between the front wheel and handlebars and the bike frame.

- Ensure that the headset is tight. Grab the brakes and try to tip the handlebars forward. No play or movement should occur outside the normal turning action. If such movement occurs, you need to tighten the headset. If you are unsure how to do this, you can research this on the Internet or take it to your local bike shop and have them show you how. A loose headset will cause damage to the head tube of the bike and ultimately be hazardous to your riding and braking capability. If you ever had a Big Wheel and an older kid bent the plastic near the steering wheel, causing the frame to sag, this is what a loose headset would be like.

- Make sure that the steering moves smoothly clockwise and counterclockwise and is not limited. If you feel any rattling, grinding, or binding, you should have the headset looked at by your local bike shop.

- Move the handlebars forward and aft to check for any play or looseness in the connections; there should be none. If you find problems here, take the time to tighten the correct bolts. If you don't know how, ask a local bike mechanic to show you how to correct this problem in the future.

FIGURE 6.2 The headset is commonly protected by a dust cover.

Seat

The seat, or saddle, is one of the most important parts on your bike in terms of comfort (see figure 6.3). Finding a good fit for your bum can require a seemingly endless search, but once you find it, it will change your world. Pay close attention to this component of your bike.

FIGURE 6.3 Be sure to find the seat that best fits your body.

- Make sure that the seat is positioned properly and check to see that it is straight. The nose of your saddle should be in line with the top tube of the bike.

- Look to ensure that the seat post has not moved up or down, affecting the seat height. If your seat is too low, you will stress your hips and lose power transfer. If your seat is too high, you will rock from side to side and create chafing or hip issues. The proper saddle height should allow your knee to open up to about 160 degrees when your foot is at the bottom of the pedal stroke. When your seat is at the correct height, your hips should remain stable and not rock up and down. If you need additional help with your seat height, your local bike shop can help you. After you find this location, properly tighten the bolt holding the seat tube in place and mark the seat tube with a marker or a small piece of electrical tape.

Tires

The tires are truly where the rubber meets the road. For that reason, let's take a little extra care in checking your tires. Some basic checks can save time, energy, and frustration in the long run.

- Visually inspect the tires to ensure they are in good condition. Look for excess wear, bald spots, and glass or other items that may be embedded in the tread (see figure 6.4*a*).

- Ensure that your tires are properly inflated. Road tires should be inflated to 120 pounds per square inch (8.3 bar) to help prevent pinch flats, which commonly occur when cyclists hit potholes or sharp bumps in the road (see figure 6.4*b*).

FIGURE 6.4   Visually inspect and fill your tires before every ride.

Chain

One thing that most people don't know is that chains (see figure 6.5) have a shelf life. Your chain can wear out or stretch, so you will need to replace it from time to time. A chain normally lasts about 2,000 to 5,000 miles (3,000 to 8,000 km) when properly cared for. Some basic care and simple checks can help ensure that you are getting the most out of your chain.

- The chain should be lubricated, but not bathed in grease. A properly functioning chain should make little to no noise and have a light amount of lubricant.
- Using a rag to clean your chain is a simple and quick fix to most problems. Follow this up with a quick spray of light bike chain lubricant and then lightly wipe the chain again. Excess grease or lubricant will act like flypaper to all the sand and grit your bike will kick up during your ride. Use a proper chain lubricant. Products

FIGURE 6.5   A clean chain is a happy chain.

like WD40 are not lubricants and will dry out your chain; this is not what you want. Ask your local bike shop for a recommendation.

- Chain stretch occurs when the links elongate slightly. Your local bike shop will have a tool that can measure this for you. Replace your chain if it becomes stretched out. A stretched chain will skip on the gears and cause frustration during your ride.

Derailleurs

Your front and rear derailleurs (see figure 6.6) are two of the most delicate pieces of equipment on your bike. Take care not to lean your bike against them. They can normally be fixed with minimal effort, but doing so takes time away from your riding.

- Inspect the front and rear derailleurs to be sure they are in good working condition. Simply shifting up and down the gears will suffice here. If you can't reach a specific gear or if skipping occurs, a simple adjustment of the cable tension can often fix the problem. This fix comes by making small turns in the barrel adjuster. We do not recommend adjusting the limit screws on the derailleurs; leave this level of adjustment to a professional mechanic.

- If you see a buildup of grit or grime, you can spray some glass cleaner on the derailleurs and wipe them clean. A short blast from an air compressor or from your mouth can also help clear obstructions from the derailleurs.

We suggest you take your bike to a trusted local bike shop at least once a year for a tune-up. You should usually do this early in the season. Don't wait until the last minute because some shops can have a 1- to 2-week waiting period for service. This kind of disruption to your training is not ideal.

FIGURE 6.6 Derailleurs: (*a*) front and (*b*) rear.

RIDING IN EXTREME WEATHER

Weather always plays a part in outdoor riding, and we usually don't recommend that you ride a road or triathlon bike outside if the temperature or windchill is below 45 degrees Fahrenheit (7 degrees Celsius). The wind on the bike can quickly drop your body temperature to an unsafe level, so it's better to be safe than out in an unexpected snow- or rainstorm. We never recommend riding in lightning, and if you are caught outside in a storm, you should immediately seek shelter in a building, restroom, gas station, or otherwise safe structure. Many cyclists are beginning to ride fat-tire bikes that have a relaxed geometry similar to a mountain bike and are designed to go over multiple kinds of terrain. These fat-tire, or snow, bikes offer a good alternative to road riding if you live in areas where snow is on the ground for more than half the year. Be sure to bundle up beforehand and know that turning the pedals on most any bike offers some level of training benefit.

HELMET

We have a simple rule we enforce with all of our athletes, friends, and children: No helmet, no ride. This rule is nonnegotiable. You never know when an accident will happen, and wearing a properly fitting helmet can save your life or the life of someone you know and love. The helmet protects your head and always needs to be in top working order. Never compromise when it comes to this important piece of protective equipment.

First, you need to be certain that your helmet fits properly (see figure 6.7). Helmets come in multiple sizes; one size doesn't fit all. When fitting a helmet, it should cover your entire skull, not just the middle to back of your head. If you are wearing sunglasses, the front should be about a centimeter above your glasses. The strap should be snug under your chin when you snap it and when the helmet is sitting properly level on your head. You should not be able to pull the strap past your chin when it is adjusted properly.

Also, check for cracks or damage to the shell or protectant foam. If you find damage, replace the helmet im-

FIGURE 6.7   Properly fitted helmet.

mediately. Cracks will compromise protection in the case of impact. Using a defective safety product is foolish. You wouldn't drive a car with a broken seatbelt or defective airbags. Why risk your safety?

Helmets do not have a defined shelf life. If the straps are secure and the helmet has no structural defects, it can last many years. But if you crash and hit your head, you should replace your helmet. Periodic cleaning with warm water and periodic replacement of the small contact pads, if your helmet has them, will improve the hygiene of the helmet. Replacements can normally be purchased at your local bike shop.

SADDLEBAG

A saddlebag is a small pouch that hangs underneath the back of your saddle. It doesn't need to be a suitcase, but it should be big enough to carry some key pieces of equipment that will help you fix any minor mechanical problems while out on the road. Suggested items include the following:

A spare tube (or two)

Tire levers to help you remove the tire from the rim

A bike small pump, commonly referred to as a micropump

CO_2 cartridges (used with an adapter to fill tires with air)

A multitool

Having the correct items in your saddlebag to repair a flat tire will ensure that you don't get stranded in the middle of nowhere. Carrying cash or a credit card comes handy when you want to stop for a snack or coffee. Cash offers an additional benefit because a dollar bill can help repair a dynamic tire failure. If you should incur a large gash in a tire, fold the dollar bill and place it between the tire and tube to fill the gash. The uniquely strong fibers in U.S. currency make it a functional bike tube repair patch. This fix may allow you to limp your bike home or to the nearest bike shop.

You should practice using all these items before you go out on the road. Being able to have a friend who can assist you in your garage is far less stressful than attempting to do something alone when you are cold and fatigued on the side of the road, far from home.

CLOTHING

Along with a good pair of bike shorts with a chamois (pad under your bum), you want to wear brightly colored clothing, such as a bike jersey, so that you are visible to other cyclists and vehicles. Although not required, a cycling jersey has pockets that come in handy for carrying essential gear such as a spare tube, a snack, or your cell phone. You can wear a bright vest over any gear so that you are extremely visible while riding out on the road.

Each day presents different weather to you and your riding friends. Dressing for the weather is important. The more often you ride, the more often you will find the need for various pieces of clothing to help you stay warm and comfortable. Some things you may look to acquiring in the future are tight-fitting base layer shirts, arm warmers, gloves, tights, beanie hats, sunglasses, light jackets, and shoe covers. The more items you have, the more often you will be able to ride outside.

ROAD-RIDING RULES

When riding on the road in traffic, you need to follow the rules of the road as if you were driving a car. You should always ride on the right side of the road so that you travel in the same direction as traffic, obey all traffic lights and signs, and use your hand signals when turning right or left to make drivers and other cyclists aware of your intentions.

Always be aware of traffic. You should never ride with ear buds because you won't be able to hear cars approaching or other sounds that you need to be aware of. Be aware that not every driver will see you or even acknowledge that you are riding a bike. We also suggest making eye contact with drivers when at a stop to be sure that they've seen you. As you ride along the right side of the road, you will be in a driver's blind spot at times. Keep back or keep at least 3 feet (1 m) between you and the vehicle if possible. Colorado and many other states require drivers to maintain 3 feet (1 m) of distance between the vehicle and a cyclist, but not everyone will adhere to the laws of the road. Occasionally, you will encounter drivers who are not thrilled to have you on the road, whether you are entitled to be there or not. In these situations it is best not to aggravate the driver; simply allow the motorist to move on. Provoking, swearing at, or arguing with a driver will often result in an outcome you do not want. When in doubt, remember the "rule of lug nuts"—he who has the most lug nuts wins. Cyclists never win in a car-versus-bike scenario. The best thing you can do is memorize the license plate of the car, get an accurate description of the driver, and report the incident to your local law enforcement. Let the police take it from there.

SHOES

Your choice of footwear will be driven by your choice of bike pedal (refer back to chapter 3 for more information about pedals). If you are riding with clipless pedals, a stiff or hard-bottomed cycling shoe that is compatible with your pedals is required. These shoes do not come with the cleat interface that mounts to the bottom, so be sure to buy the correct cleat for your pedals when buying your shoes. If you are using platform pedals, you can simply ride in your running shoes, but hard-bottomed cycling shoes offer the advantage of preventing fatigue in your arches or feet during sustained hard pedaling efforts.

Your bike shoe should fit comfortably with a thin sock, but it should also allow room for a heavier sock in colder weather. We talked about shoes in chapter 3, but it's worth mentioning again that you're going to need to decide whether it is beneficial to purchase tri-specific shoes (shoes with one or two straps). The basic difference is in the number of fastening straps and the structural design of the shoe. Tri-specific shoes allow you to get in and out of them quickly (even while riding the bike!), so the tongue of the shoe may be modified or nonexistent and the rear heel cup may be shorter or smaller.

Cycling Skills

Cycling skills are essential to your training, safety, comfort, and racing. If you are a bronze- or silver-level cyclist, you likely have not ridden a bike for several years and are a little nervous about braving the roads. We suggest you start on a bike path or in an empty parking lot to practice key bike-handling skills. Practicing these skills may sound silly and remedial, but we like to say, "Better safe than sorry." Even if you are a gold-level cyclist, you should freshen up your riding skills before you start training for the triathlon.

RIDING IN A STRAIGHT LINE

You need to be able to ride in a straight line, hold your line, and be able to go around corners safely. Whether going straight or around a corner, holding your line allows those around you to know where you will be going. This predictability is key to preventing riders from bumping into each other and allowing them to ride safely from point to point as fast as possible.

Hop on your bike and practice following a painted line in a parking lot, staying on the line as long as you can (see figure 6.8a), and periodically looking back over your shoulder for a second or two (see figure 6.8b). You will need to do this often during a race to check for cars or other cyclists. Beginners often swerve the bike as they turn their heads. You want to maintain the straight line while you look back. A trick to making your riding more relaxed is to keep your eyes about 50 yards (m) up the road. Presumably, you drive a car during your nontraining times. In drivers education your instructor likely discussed where to focus on the road when you are driving. By focusing up the road you open up your field of view and allow yourself more time to react to obstacles because you will notice them before they create an emergency in your path of travel. For the same reasons, you should focus your field of view up the road while biking. You will be able to ride safer for all the same reasons, and your old drivers ed teacher will be proud.

a

b

FIGURE 6.8 Riding straight is sometimes easier said than done; it is best to practice in a safe area.

CORNERING

After you are comfortable riding in a straight line, you are ready to practice cornering (see figure 6.9). To maintain speed, you can lean your bike into the direction of the corner you are taking. Many accidents occur during cornering, so you need to understand the capabilities of your bike. Normally, your bike can offer you only 100 percent of itself. If you ask for or apply 50 percent of the bike's braking capabilities, you will be able to use only 50 percent of the bike's turning abilities. This means you should slow down and brake as you approach a corner so that you can turn most effectively when you need to.

FIGURE 6.9 Cornering.

Keep your balance evenly over the bike during the turn. Keep your hands on the shifters or hoods, never on the pads of aerobars. Pedal placement is also vital to preventing crashes. Push the outside pedal down and keep the inside pedal high or at the top of the pedal stroke during every turn to ensure that your pedals never contact the ground. Then, as you round the corner, lean in and let the bike roll through. After you are through the turn, you can pedal several times to regain your momentum. Again, if you haven't been on a bike in a long time, you should practice cornering skills in an empty parking lot until you feel comfortable going out on a bike path or the road.

BRAKING

Many triathletes just starting out overdo the brakes. Grabbing too much of the front brake will send you flying over your handlebars. Instead, you want to feather or gradually increase pressure on both the front and rear brakes at the same time to slow down while approaching a stop sign or stoplight. Feathering the brakes will not only offer you a more comfortable riding experience but also, if you are riding with others, allow riders behind you to slow down safely and slowly. While descending, you will want to feather the front brake lightly while holding consistent pressure on the rear brake with your weight shifted back over the seat to help you maintain control of your bike. If you must brake quickly to avoid a car door, dog, bear, or other obstacle, evenly apply pressure to both brakes at the same time. This even application of braking power will ensure the fastest, most balanced stopping that your bike can produce.

Keep in mind that one of the most vital and underused skill in braking is awareness of your surroundings. Keep your senses sharp by always looking around and hearing noises in your area. If you can anticipate a braking scenario, you can often do it with less stress and urgency.

SHIFTING

Shifting your bike skillfully can help you tremendously during a race. Learning how to shift into a lower gear before climbing a big hill or going through a sharp corner will save you time and save your chain ring from unnecessary stress. A typical bike has between 18 and 30 gears to use. You'll want to avoid putting your chain in the biggest chain ring in the front and the biggest sprocket in the back. This configuration, called cross-chaining, is really hard on your drivetrain. Cross-chaining creates binding and torque that your chain is not designed to withstand. A newer chain may have no issues during this cross-chaining, but a weak or older chain is more likely to snap when used in this gear ratio.

Before you shift, especially as you approach a hill, you should ease up on your pedaling a bit, shift the bike into an easier gear, and then resume your normal pedal cadence. This practice can help prevent you from dropping the chain. If you try to shift while in a hard gear under a heavy load, the chain may pop off and you'll have to stop and put it back on. When you are at the top of the hill, you should again ease off your pedal stroke, shift into a harder gear, and ride down the hill in your big chain ring. Your bike has many gears, so use them. Think of your bike like a car. As you drive up a mountain, you shift gears to maintain a desired number of RPMs. As you descend, you shift accordingly to maintain the same level. Do the same with your bike. Manipulate the gears so that you always ride between 85 and 95 RPMs.

CLIPPING IN AND UNCLIPPING

If you are a bronze-level cyclist, you'll most likely just wear your running shoes on top of platform pedals on your bike. If you are a silver- or gold-level cyclist, you can get the most power from your pedal stroke with clipless pedals and cycling-specific shoes. Learning how to clip and unclip your cycling shoes to and from your pedals will help prevent you from falling over when you need to stop or start on your bike.

Clipping in is normally easily learned, but a few key points can help here. First, always keep your eyes forward when clipping in. Dropping your eyes to your feet while you are clipping in will inevitably result in your running off the road or into someone else. Feel the cleat with your foot and begin to understand the relationship of where your foot needs to go to be centered on your pedal. If you find that your shoe is not clicking in easily, slightly move your foot around to work into the cleat. If you can't seem to get your foot in, don't worry. Just push down on the pedals a few times to keep your momentum and try again. With a little practice, clipping in will become second nature.

When riding during normal circumstances, you should unclip your right foot about 30 to 40 feet (about 10 m) before stopping to prepare to place your foot on the ground for balance. Keep your left foot clipped in so that you need to clip only one foot into the pedal as your begin to move forward again. During a race you should unclip a bit earlier, about 75 yards (m) before you expect to stop and dismount. This longer unclipping period is recommended because of the possibility of your needing to stop earlier for some unexpected reason, such as a person falling or braking hard in front of you. Practicing clipping in and unclipping is key to proficient execution.

A grassy field or your indoor cycling trainer is a good place to practice clipping in and unclipping. Put on your bike shoes, put one shoe in the pedal, and then start pedaling a bit. After you have a little speed you

GETTING THE PROPER BIKE FIT

To be comfortable and to get the most out of your bike riding and training, we suggest you get a professional bike fit either at the shop where you bought the bike or from a certified bike fitter. Reputable bike fit certifications include Retul, F.I.S.T., and Serotta Cycling Institute. By being positioned correctly, you not only get the most power possible out of pedaling but also avoid back, neck, or knee pain. A properly fitted bike can make all the difference in the world when you are training and racing. You should avoid riding a bike that is too small or too large for you. You can also use an online bike-fitting tool to help. A few simple measurements can help you get set up:

Height: _____ cm

Sternal notch height: _____ cm

Inseam length: _____ cm

Thigh length: _____ cm

Arm length: _____ cm

Shoulder width: _____ cm

Foot length: _____ cm

Saddle height over handlebar: _____ cm

Figure 6.10 provides a visual to help you know where exactly on your bike to measure.

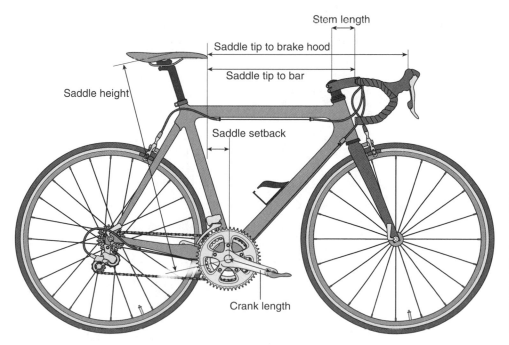

FIGURE 6.10 Bike measurements.

After you have your measurements, you should record those numbers so that you can replicate the settings later.

can work your other bike shoe into the pedal. For unclipping, you can always unclip one foot while you are slowing down, touch that foot to the ground when you stop, and then unclip the other foot.

GROUP RIDING AND ETIQUETTE

A skill that you will develop as you progress in your training is group riding. This skill allows you to ride comfortably within 1 foot (30 cm) of the riders around you. Skills to focus on for good group-riding etiquette are those that we've covered previously—holding your line, feathering your brakes, and signaling road hazards.

If you are a bronze- or silver-level cyclist, you should probably practice riding with a small group of friends or a beginner cycling group before joining a large group ride with pro-level cyclists. You'll want to learn basic group cycling etiquette from people who don't intimidate you.

If you are a gold-level cyclist, you can ride in groups when doing so is appropriate in your training program. Consider, for example, how comfortable you are when following behind another cyclist. In a group ride, cyclists ride close to the wheel of the rider in front of them to get the most draft and save energy. You have to be alert in case the person in front of you slows the pace, moves to avoid a pothole or other obstacle, or needs to stop suddenly. You also need to learn how to ride in a pace line, taking turns pulling at the front (see figure 6.11). In a pace

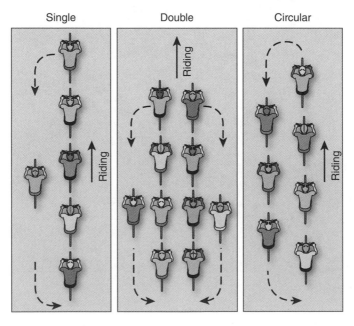

FIGURE 6.11   Riding in a pace line.

line, each rider rides at the front of the group for a certain period and then slowly moves left, drifts to the back of the line, and catches the wheel of the last rider in the line. If you go out riding with cyclists of similar ability, you will find it easier to keep up the pace and stay within the pack. Falling off the back is called being dropped. Some group rides will go on without you; others will stop at designated locations and wait for everyone to catch up.

You also need to understand hand signals and use them while riding in a group. A rider in front of you pointing to something, such as a rock, pothole, or other debris, is your warning not to ride over the obstacle. A rider in front of you putting an open hand behind the middle of the back is a warning to slow down because the group is going to stop. Riders give signals for right and left hand turns as well. You need to learn these signals and use them for the riders behind you. Be aware that riders may execute some of these signals in different ways. Before a ride you may want to have a quick chat with your fellow riders about what signals will be used. An oral announcement should accompany each of these signals to ensure that everyone knows what you are pointing at or going to do. Here are a few common signals:

- **Left turn**: point to the left with the left hand (see figure 6.12*a*)
- **Right turn**: point to the right with the right hand (see figure 6.12*b*)
- **Slowing**: hold out the right arm with the elbow bent 90 degrees and the hand pointed toward the ground (see figure 6.12*c*)
- **Stopping**: hold out the right arm with elbow bent 90 degrees and the hand pointed upward (see figure 6.12*d*)
- **Road obstacle**: point at the obstacle on the ground (see figure 6.12*e*)

CYCLING WARM-UP

Before you start any bike training, you want to make sure to warm up your muscles. If you are riding outside, the easiest way to do this is to head out on a relatively flat road and spin easily for about 10 minutes. This activity will get your legs activated and ready to ride. If you are riding on an indoor trainer or indoor bike, you can start in an easy gear and spin your legs for about 10 minutes before starting your workout.

FIGURE 6.12 Cycling hand signals: (*a*) left turn, (*b*) right turn, (*c*) slowing, (*d*) stopping, and (*e*) road obstacle.

Cycling Training

As with training for swimming, each cycling workout needs to have a purpose. If you go out and just ride your bike leisurely, you won't make the fitness gains you want to see before your first race. At the same time, you want to make sure you aren't riding so hard each time that you can't recover. Each training ride should have a warm-up, main objective, and cool-down. We will discuss specific cycling workouts in the chapter on training plans later in the book. Although riders will have varying training needs and objectives, here are a few general training principles we would like to cover.

To become a better cyclist and become more fit on the bike, a bronze-level athlete should aim to ride a minimum of 3 days per week for an average of 30 to 45 minutes per workout. A silver- or gold-level athlete should try to ride 3 to 4 days per week for an average of 45 to 60 minutes per session. An experienced rider can ride 4 to 5 days per week, averaging 60 to 75 minutes per ride. No matter which level of athlete you are, you should try to divide your overall time on the bike into three main workout types:

Recovery Workouts

Recovery workouts, also known as active recovery or easy riding, are designed to be executed at an easy level to help your body rebuild after harder workouts. You will feel more refreshed and ready for your next workout after performing a light workout than you would by recovering with no activity. By not being active, your muscles will feel tight and fatigue will weigh you down mentally. You will have a more difficult time getting things going for your next workout. About 25 percent of your training should be spent doing recovery workouts. Your heart rate should stay in zones 1 or 2, your rate of perceived exertion (RPE) should be under 10, and you should be able to hold casual conversations during recovery workouts. Your RPE is a scale used to determine your rate of perceived exertion during exercise (for a deeper understanding of heart rate zones, see "Calculating Your Heart Rate" in chapter 7). The RPE scale runs from 0 to 10 with 0 being the least amount of perceived exertion and 10 being the highest amount of perceived exertion.

Drill and Interval Workouts

Drills and interval workouts are the way in which you get most of the hard stuff done. The focus is on high-intensity effort and technique development. In these workouts you are pushing yourself to the limits, either physically or mentally. These high-intensity, lower-volume workouts focus on specific aspects of speed and technique. They normally make up 15 percent of your total training time. Many athletes make the mistake of spending more time in this style of training but at a lower level of intensity. For intervals and speed workouts, you benefit more by spending less time at higher intensity. A rule of thumb we have is to make the hard stuff hard and the easy stuff easy. When we say hard, we are referring to a maximal effort for the time in the interval. In these workouts you will see your maximum heart rate and should be at a RPE of 8 or 9.

Endurance Workouts

Endurance workouts are designed to be done just below threshold to build your aerobic base. You should be able to do them for a longer time but still feel a bit of fatigue. You should be able to hold one- to two-sentence conversations during the efforts, and your RPE should be 7 to 8. You should do about 60 percent of your workouts as endurance training.

Within these three styles of workouts, we can further define what types of training you can do during each segment. We can further define the training done in the speed and technique segments into specific workouts including hill climbing, power workouts, skill development, and bike handling. The type of cycling training you need to do depends on several factors including the racecourse, the terrain where you live, and the climate where you live. If you live in a coastal town in south Florida, doing 10-minute hill repeats outside will be difficult. In that case, you could move your hill-climbing workouts to an indoor trainer if you have access to one. On the other hand, if you live in a mountain community in Colorado, you may not have a flat place for a recovery ride, so you may need to move those indoors to ensure proper recovery.

TRAVELING AND CYCLING

If you have to travel for business and are staying in a chain hotel, you can still continue your cycling training. Most hotels offer a gym, and most have a few indoor bikes, usually recumbent bikes or upright bikes. Either will do the trick when you want to do a few cycling training sessions while traveling. If you don't have access to a bike, you'll have to adjust your training for that period to do more swimming and running instead. If you are going on a family trip by car and can take your bike for a few workouts, you can maintain cycling fitness while traveling. We discussed flying with your bike and the associated costs. Another option to consider is renting a bike when you are traveling and exploring the area while doing your cycling workouts. Most bike shops have a road bike rental option in the $50 per day range.

Preparing for the Race

During most races, you will be getting on your bike in transition 1 (T1), right after finishing the swim. You should practice the transition routine during your training cycle. You'll have to spend a few minutes to gather yourself, pull off your wetsuit, and put on your helmet, sunglasses, and cycling shoes, but the key is to select a specific series of steps that are comfortable to you and to repeat them slowly and accurately until they become smooth. After you become comfortable with this routine, speed it up a bit. Practicing the transition will help when you are disoriented or cold. Here are a few tips for T1:

- If the water is cold, you might want to use a towel to dry off a bit so that you don't cool down quickly on the ride.

- We suggest that you take the time to dry your feet and put on a good pair of racing socks to prevent blisters on the bike and the run. Some athletes put baby powder in their shoes to make it easier to put them on with damp feet.

- Keep your transition area minimalistic. The more clutter you have, the more opportunities you will have to encounter a problem. Streamline to the essentials.

- Don't bring a water bucket. Your feet are going to be dirty; accept it. If you have sand on your toes, use a towel to wipe them down. Water buckets splash all over your items and often tip over, soaking everyone around you.

- Think through the steps the night before. Mentally walk through the steps you will take in T1 and memorize them. You don't want to leave without your helmet or ride in your wetsuit. Trust us; we have seen that happen more than once.

Also, to ensure a good T1, spend a few minutes before starting the race to ensure that you have your bike in a proper gear for beginning the race. If you will encounter a large hill right away, shift the gears into an easy gear. Make sure that your water bottles are filled and securely seated into their cages. Having a bottle pop out as you run through transition or ride down the road can be a disaster. Most races do not offer aid in the form of hydration or nutrition out on the course, so be sure not to lose what you are taking.

You'll need to run your bike out of transition to the mount line, which is a line right outside transition that you must cross before you can get on your bike and ride. The line will be flagged, marked with cones, and staffed by volunteers. Be cautious around other athletes so that you don't run into anyone or cause a pileup at the often-chaotic mount line. It's OK to move over to the side where you are more comfortable and can take your time to get on safely.

After you get on your bike, it's time to ride. Remember that most races are not draft legal, so always keep three bike lengths between you and the other racers. If you are a slower rider, you should ride toward the right side of the road so that others can pass you safely on your left-hand side. If you plan to pass someone, always pass on the left, but only when it is safe to do so. Announce to the other rider, "On your left" as you go by. You then need to ride fast enough to pass safely and put yourself three bike lengths ahead of the rider you went by. If you don't do this, you will be penalized by the race officials.

Racecourses have a mixture of fully closed areas and areas that will have open and flowing street traffic. All USAT-sanctioned races are required to have law enforcement officers and volunteers at intersections to control the flow of traffic. If you are choosing to participate in a nonsanctioned event, be aware that these safety precautions may not be in place. Slow down accordingly to avoid any possibility of having a collision with a vehicle (remember the rule of lug nuts).

After you have completed the bike portion of the race, prepare to slow down as you ride back into transition 2 (T2). Dismount your bike before you reach the dismount line, which is labeled, flagged, and staffed with volunteers to ensure that all racers get safely off their bikes. After you dismount, you can run with your bike, holding it by the seat or handlebars, back to your transition spot and rack it. Only after you have racked your bike should you remove your helmet. At this point in T2, you can switch into running shoes if you wore cycling shoes for the cycling portion of the race, grab your bib or race belt, and put on a hat or visor. You are off to the final portion of the race, the run, which we will cover in the next chapter.

CHAPTER 7

RUNNING

Now that you have completed the swim portion of the race, you will prepare for the final segment of your race, the run. In this chapter we discuss running cadence, form, dynamic warm-ups, run training, and conditions.

Running Skills

Running is one of those activities that all of us think we know how to do, but unfortunately, many times we are doing it wrong. Let's look at how we can reverse that and turn running into a lifelong sport.

RUN CADENCE

From a triathlon perspective, we need to understand the effect that the bike portion of race has on the third leg of the race. Ideally, you will have biked with an efficient pedal stroke at around 90 RPM during the bike segment of the race. This effort will have set up your legs for the transition into the optimal run cadence of 90 foot strikes per minute. When done properly over time, this pace of foot strike will become second nature, but for now we will focus on how to practice this in training.

If you own a gadget that tracks your run cadence, focus on that number and aim for our desired number of 90. If you don't have such a device or if you are having trouble syncing up with the magic number of 90, try this trick. Download a simple and free metronome app to your phone or favorite mobile device. Plug in a set of headphones and set the app to 90 beats per minute. Set a treadmill to a moderate speed for your ability and focus on matching your foot strikes to the tempo of the beat. You may need a little practice, so be sure to start slow. You will likely have to play around with your stride length to get the timing down.

Another gadget you may already have that can help here is a tempo trainer normally used for swimming. This silver-dollar-sized gadget, which you clip to your hat or visor, supplies you with a rhythm or tempo. Note here that many coaches discourage running or training with headphones playing music because the music tempo can affect your foot strike tempo. For this reason, we encourage you to retire the headphones for your training until you get the tempo locked in.

RUNNING FORM

Now that you have the timing down, let's focus on your running form. Proper running form helps you conserve energy while moving, increases lung performance, and prevents unnecessary fatigue of your head, neck, and shoulders that could ultimately slow you down. By maintaining proper alignment and position as we discuss here, you'll be able to finish the run portion of your race in good form and good spirits.

Body Position

While running, keep your head and neck up and focus your eyes approximately 2 to 3 feet (60 to 90 cm) out ahead of you. Your upper body and shoulders are relaxed, the core is engaged, and the spine is in a slight forward lean. Your arms are bent at a 90-degree angle. Keep them close to your body and do not cross them in front of your body as you run. Hands are in a soft fist, and your thumbs are on top of your fists. Your hips and pelvis should be stable and move in a horizontal plane while your legs help create forward momentum. See figure 7.1 for an example of proper running form.

Foot Strike

Running and walking are two naturally occurring methods of transportation that the body develops from infancy. As children, we achieve most of our motion by running. But many parents go about day-to-day life frustrated from telling their kids to slow down and not run, whether in the house, in school, in the mall, or into the street. As we age, we become more sedentary, and walking becomes our primary method of transportation. We run less, and when we do it, it's not for the same reasons we had when we were children. This point has an influence on how we run. As children we are not taught how to run; we do it because our bodies know what to do. If you watch a child run, you will see a natural fluid midfoot

FIGURE 7.1 Proper running form.

strike along with functional arm swing. The body was designed to absorb impact and propel itself forward quickly. Walking is fundamentally different. A walking step lands in front of the body's center of gravity, rocks over the midfoot, and pushes off the back at an angle equal to where it landed in the front. Over time and because of a lot of misinformation circulated in the 1970s during the marathon boom, most adults were told that the way they walk was supposed to be the same way they run. This misconception caused most of the running injuries over the last 40 years.

Your foot normally strikes the ground with about three times the force of your body weight during an average running stride. For a 200-pound (90 kg) runner, each foot needs to absorb 600 pounds (27 kg) every time it lands. If the foot lands in front of the body's center of gravity, the impact point becomes the heel and the mechanics of the leg are such that the ankle is at a 90-degree angle and the knee is locked out straight. Because the ankle and the knee joints are not absorbing any impact, most of it is left to be absorbed by the product in the heel of your running shoe. Because the impact cannot be completely absorbed by that product, it reverberates up through the tibia and fibula, across the cartilage of the locked knee joint, and through the femur and pelvis, eventually ending up in the lower back. This method of absorbing impact is not sustainable long term. Your bones and joints were not designed to absorb impact in this manner.

By simply moving the foot under the center of the body's gravity and allowing the midfoot to strike the ground (see figure 7.2), you create an entirely different model of impact absorption. In this position the ankle is able to flex along with the knee as the impact of the body hits the ground. The hypothetical 600 pounds (270 kg) is now absorbed by the muscles in the foot and the legs. The joints simply facilitate motion, and the bones essentially provide stability.

When you improperly strike the ground with the heel, the muscles do not provide much more than some functional movement for the skeleton.

FIGURE 7.2 Center of gravity foot strike.

RUNNING WARM-UP

Before starting any run, you need to activate your muscles by doing a short dynamic warm-up. If you can spend even 5 or 10 minutes before each run, your muscles will be activated, warmed up, and ready to go. If you are short on time, choose two from the following list. You need to have great posture, tighten your abs, and focus on what you are doing. Effective dynamic running drills include the following:

- **Butt kicks**: With good posture, start jogging in place. As you're jogging, emphasize your back stride, bring your heel to your butt, and try to make contact between your heel and your butt. If you can't reach, don't worry. Just bring your heel up as far as you can.

- **Carioca**: Move sideways with your arms out and cross right over left, right behind left, right over left. Repeat by starting with the left foot first: left over right, left behind right, left over right. Move in one direction for 10 seconds, switch directions, and repeat.

- **Knee hugs**: Standing with good posture, grab one knee with both hands and raise it toward your chest while firing your glutes in your anchor to maintain your balance. Release your knee and step forward with that leg, alternating legs while you walk forward. Do 10 on each side.

- **Heel walks**: Walk forward with your weight on your heels, flexing your feet so that the balls of your feet are off the ground for 20 to 30 seconds. This drill activates your shin muscles while stretching out your calves.

- **Forward skip**: Jog slowly while skipping forward for 20 to 30 seconds. Repeat three times.

- **Jumping jacks**: Stand with good posture with your arms and legs together. Jump so that your arms and legs are apart. Repeat 10 to 15 times.

But when you use a midfoot strike, the muscles absorb the load of the impact and propel the body forward. Thus, strengthening the muscles to endure impact over a longer time (endurance training) becomes a logical function of our training. A by-product of a proper midfoot strike is that you are now less likely to incur bone fractures and joint damage from repeated impact absorption as you would when you strike the ground with the heel first. Using a midfoot strike is how you turn running into a lifelong sport, not just a young person's game.

You can use several techniques to learn the midfoot style of running. We do not endorse any particular style or brand of training. Remember that in the process of relearning how to run properly, you must approach the transition from heel striking to midfoot striking with caution and patience. By converting too quickly, you will experience an overload in your calves and quads, which can lead to other injuries. A gradual approach lasting for 6 to 10 weeks along with strength-training movements like calf raises and lunges will help develop the muscle endurance your body needs to readapt to its old running style.

Run Training

In this section we discuss how to increase your run volume and run progression. If you are a bronze- or silver-level runner, you want to progress your training slowly and safely. We discuss the various types of run workouts that you will be doing each week and the benefits of mixing up your running workouts and terrain. We also discuss how to perform a brick workout and what you can expect physically when you do that type of workout.

RUN PROGRESSION

After you have learned proper running mechanics and form, you can begin to add more volume. A safe rule of thumb is to increase run volume by only 10 percent every 2 weeks. For example, if you run a total of 10 miles per week, when you decide to increase your run volume, you will run 10 total miles the first week, 11 miles the second, and 12 the third. This rule should apply not only to a single long run but also to total weekly run volume. If your long run is 5 miles, then the following week you can increase it to 5.5 miles, and then 6 miles the next week. By increasing volume too rapidly, you risk injury by not allowing your body to adapt to the greater level of stress that comes from absorbing the impact of each stride. By the same reasoning, you should not begin to incorporate speed or track workouts until you have established a solid base of running, which can take 8 to 12 weeks.

When planning a run progression in your training plan, we recommend starting with a base, incorporating speed, and then focusing on endurance to achieve optimal performance results. To establish a base for your run training, you can alternate running and walking (1-minute run, 1-minute walk) 3 days per week until you can run for 20 to 30 consecutive minutes.

After you establish a base, a typical week would start with a shorter, lower-intensity recovery run at an easy aerobic level. Bronze-level runners would run for 20 to 30 minutes, and silver- and gold-level runners would run for 30 to 40 minutes. Athletes often skip or incorrectly execute this run because they often don't see the purpose of running slowly or think they need to make up for a previous workout. This workout is beneficial because you have ideally done a weekly long run on the prior weekend when your body has absorbed its highest volume of stress. As the body recovers, it needs a chance to breathe and rest, assisted by light movement and exercise. If you don't allow the body to recover or rest properly, you begin the countdown to injury.

Your next run, the midweek run, should incorporate a variable pace, variable terrain, or a bit of speed. You should run for 30 minutes if you are a bronze-level runner and 30 to 45 minutes if you are a silver- or gold-level runner. Varying your speed or incorporating fartlek running is a good way to bring a little variety into your running. Runners often make the mistake of always running at the same speed in the same grey zone of training. They are never running hard enough to make advancements in speed and never running slow enough to allow the body to recover or rest actively. For these midweek runs, ensure that you are executing these harder efforts above your normal comfort level. The goal is to raise your heart rate and begin acclimating your muscles to the demands of running faster. After each interval, slow down and let your heart rate recover. During these recovery periods you can walk or jog slowly—either is acceptable—but you should allow your heart rate to settle down before you start another interval. Running on trails or other soft surfaces gives your body a way to adapt to absorbing impact on more than just concrete or pavement. The surface variations will ultimately strengthen your feet, giving you a better chance of avoiding injury should you hit any unforeseen obstacles on your next run.

The last run of the week should be your long run. The duration of the long run will vary according to your ability and your goal. If you are a bronze-level runner, the run might be 45 to 50 minutes. If you are a silver- or gold-level runner, 50 to 60 minutes is long enough if you are training for a sprint-distance race. These runs are meant to be a little faster than your easy runs, but not as fast as midweek runs. They should normally be conversational in pace, meaning that you should be able to hold a conversation while running. You should be able to speak a short sentence without stopping to breathe. Doing this run with a friend can help break up the monotony of the workout and keep you motivated. You might also choose to join a running group that can give you support and motivation on the weekend. Look to your local running store or tri shop for available options in your area. Also, for your long runs, think ahead and bring some water and some form of nutrition like a sports gel in case you begin to run low on energy (we talk more about this later). After your long run, spend at least 10 minutes stretching. Stretching after you exercise helps alleviate tight muscles and allows

CALCULATING YOUR HEART RATE

One of the most widely used methods of measuring your training intensity is monitoring your heart rate. Heart rate training or HR training has been around for many years, but the methodology around defining your specific HR zones and the basic structure of those zones has been a commonly debated issue for many years. For the purpose of simplification we are going to use a common five zone platform. We will define our zones based on percentages of your maximum heart rate. Your Max HR is the highest your HR can physically go. This number varies from person to person and can increase or decrease throughout your life based on age, fitness level, illness, or altitude. Defining your maximum HR can be done fairly easily, but beware, you are going to have to break a sweat.

The first thing we recommend is the purchase of an HR monitor. There are many styles and models on the market, but all you really need is a basic model that consists of a watch style display and chest strap. Once you have your HR monitor you're ready to define your max HR. Before doing this test, we recommend you speak with your doctor and be sure this is safe for you. Assuming all systems are go, map out a course or use a track where you can run uninterrupted for three minutes or more. Begin with a 10 minute easy warm up jog. Add 3, 20 second accelerations with 90 second rest intervals at the end to help you prepare. After you are warmed up, run as fast as you can for three minutes. Keep the pace as even as you can, then jog easy for two minutes. Let your HR come down and catch your breath. After the two minute easy jog, run as hard as you can for three minutes once more. During this second interval keep tabs on your HR and remember the highest it peaks. This number will be your max HR. Cool down with a 60 second walk and 5 minute easy jog. Now that you have your max HR, you can set your HR zones. Using your max HR calculate your zones based on the following percentages: zone 1 = 0 to 60 percent, zone 2 = 60 to 75 percent, zone 3 = 75 to 85 percent, zone 4 = 85 to 95 percent, zone 5 = 95 to 100 percent.

Two other ways to determine your HR zones are with a metabolic cart and by using your age. The first method, the metabolic cart, is a test that will most likely be done in a lab or under the supervision of a doctor. It will involve an interment in which you breathe in and out of during the test. It will monitor the oxygen content of your breath as you inhale and exhale. Because it involves a mask, some find this style test to be very claustrophobic. This test however is the industry standard for accurately determining your aerobic threshold or the point where your body can no longer supply the amount of oxygen it is consuming. Using this number, your HR zones can be established by the technician or your coach. The second and most commonly used method of establishing HR zones is by defining your max HR by taking 220 and subtracting your age. This is a simple method and widely used because it is fast, easy, and doesn't require any work. The problem with this method is that it has an error rate of approximately 20 beats per minute. This error rate makes this method not as desirable for us and so we do not recommend it.

your body to cool down slowly. If you are not finishing near your home, bring a small snack of 200 to 300 calories to help refuel. One of the worst things you can do after a long run is to starve your body by not refueling after you finish. The average body burns approximately 600 calories per hour while running at an aerobic pace. Don't hurt yourself by not properly refilling the tank. You don't need to go out and eat a slab of bacon or three orders of pancakes, but you should play it smart. Have a snack with some fruit and protein and plenty of water to refuel and recover for your next workout.

If you are a silver- or gold-level runner, you can run 4 days per week by adding an extra aerobic run. If you use a heart rate monitor, this easy run should be in zone 1. If you do not have a heart rate monitor, try limiting yourself to breathing only in and out of your nose. If you find the need to breathe out of your mouth, slow down. If you have to walk at times, that is OK.

BRICK WORKOUTS

On some days you may be biking before you run, either by design or by happenstance. If you do this by design, you are doing what is called a brick workout. The origin of the term *brick workout* is unknown, but popular speculation attributes it to the phrase *bike, run, ick*, meaning that your legs feel icky or that after biking, your legs feel like bricks. Either way, you will definitely benefit by acclimating to the feeling of running right off the bike. Incorporating your midweek run to coincide with a preceding bike ride can offer multiple benefits. First, you begin to understand how your body and legs feel when moving immediately from one sport to another. This acclimation will allow you to overcome the mental aspect of simply wanting to walk right off the bike. You also begin to find motivation in how to push through the "ick" and get into a consistent run cadence.

Brick workouts do not necessarily need to be a single bike followed by a single run. You can break up this workout to create a fun training session by doing short bike intervals followed by short run intervals. This approach is also an excellent way to practice your second transition (T2) technique. Set up your bike in your garage, along with a small towel, your running shoes, a hat or visor, and maybe a water bottle. Bike for 5 to 10 minutes around your neighborhood, return to your garage, and slowly change from your biking equipment to your running equipment. Many race videos on the Internet show how athletes do this. The goal is to find a personal rhythm and stick with that. The important point here is not to unclip your helmet until you have placed your bike firmly on the bike rack or leaned it against the wall of your garage. Remember, start slowly and think through the steps. Run for 3 to 5 minutes and return to the bike. Repeat the same pattern but imagine that you are coming out of the water. Do this several times, speeding up the routine as you go. Before you know it, you will be flying through the process with ease and skill.

Preparing for the Race

Because you will likely be completing your first triathlon during the summer in the heat, you should practice running in all types of conditions, including rain and heat, so that your body can adjust to the conditions on race day. If you run in the rain, having the proper rain gear, such as a light rain jacket that keeps you dry underneath, is essential. We don't promote running during a thunderstorm, but a nice spring rain or sprinkle isn't going to hurt you and will build your confidence and mental toughness for race day when conditions may be less than ideal. Running in the heat is another element of training that you should practice before your race. If possible, try running during the middle of the day or late afternoon for at least one of your weekly run workouts to practice the pacing and hydration needed on a hot day. A few things to consider during a run in the heat include wearing waterproof or sweatproof sunscreen, wearing a hat or visor, putting cold water or a cold-water sponge on your head to keep cool, increasing your fluid intake, possibly using a sports drink on longer runs, wearing light, breathable clothing, and wearing a sweatband to help absorb the sweat.

––––––––––––––––

You will find that we have built many of these running elements into the training plans that are found later in the book, but as you progress in the sport of triathlon, never lose sight of the fundamental running elements we have spoken about. With a foundation of good technique and a sound base of endurance, you will see the improvement you desire. Now that we have covered the swim, bike, run, T1, and T2, we move into strength training for triathletes.

PART III

TRAINING

TRAINING PLAN KEY

Swim Key

BLD—build (stronger and faster within the swim distance)

CH—choice (any stroke, drill, kick, and so on)

DPS—distance per stroke (extending so that you are one or two strokes fewer than normal per lap)

DR—drill

EZ—easy (recovery or cool-down)

F—fast (go as fast as you can)

FR—freestyle

IM—individual medley (butterfly, backstroke, breaststroke, and freestyle)

K—kick (with or without a kickboard)

NF—nonfreestyle (butterfly, backstroke, breaststroke, or IM)

P—pull (using buoy or paddles)

RB—restricted breathing (breathing every three to five strokes)

S—swim (any stroke)

SC—scull

Bike Key

Easy aerobic—easy pace using nasal breathing (heart rate zone: 165 minus age in years)

Aerobic—stronger pace but can talk easily (heart rate zone: 170 minus age in years)

Strong aerobic—legs feel fatigue but can hold for 30 to 50 miles (50 to 80 km) (heart rate zone: 180 minus age in years)

Run Key

Easy aerobic—easy pace using nasal breathing (heart rate zone: 165 minus age in years)

Aerobic—stronger pace but can talk easily (heart rate zone: 170 minus age in years)

Strong aerobic—typical half-marathon effort (heart rate zone: 185 minus age in years)

CHAPTER **8**

STRENGTH AND FLEXIBILITY

So far, we have discussed the importance of skills and drills for the swim, the bike, and the run. We now shift our focus to another key aspect of training for triathlon—strength and flexibility. We realize you are busy swimming, biking, and running, but adding some basic strength-training exercises into your training plan 2 or 3 days per week for 20 to 30 minutes will make you stronger and help prevent injuries.

In triathlon we suggest that athletes think about the movement in each exercise they do. Because your time is valuable, you don't want to do any exercises that may not benefit you in the sport of triathlon. We want you to think about how the exercises we have chosen and any others that you may choose to add are specific to motions executed in triathlon. If an exercise does not function in a manner in which you move in swimming, biking, or running, ask yourself whether it is beneficial. You want to do sport-specific exercises that help you go faster, become stronger, and become injured less frequently. Sport-specific exercises vary according to which triathlon sport you are doing. For example, because you use your shoulders a lot during swimming, an exercise such as the shoulder press would be considered sport specific. In cycling, you use your quadriceps a lot, so an exercise such as squats would be considered sport specific. And for running, you use your quadriceps and hamstrings a lot, so lunges would be sport specific.

In this chapter we discuss how strength training can help you, and how you can incorporate the sessions into your busy training schedule. We show you 16 exercises that build strength and explain the equipment you will need to perform those exercises. Lastly, we describe movements to improve flexibility and explain why flexibility is important for triathletes.

Benefits of Strength Training

Although you may find several benefits to performing strength-training exercises, we focus here on the key benefits that will help you in your triathlon training.

INCREASE PERFORMANCE

The stronger you are, the faster you can become. If you can swim, bike, and run faster, then ultimately you can race faster. Becoming faster may not be your number one goal at this time, but it is something to keep in mind for the future, after you've completed your first triathlon and decide to do another one! Be aware that just because you have more muscle, you may not necessarily be faster. Overdevelopment of muscle can restrict flexibility. For example, having large shoulder muscles can restrict the range of motion in your swim stroke. Therefore, we will discuss why flexibility is important and how you can incorporate it into your routine.

RESOLVE MUSCLE IMBALANCES

Muscles imbalances often result from preforming repetitive exercises that use the same muscle groups. For example, if you are a bronze-level runner and a gold-level cyclist, you may have weaker hamstrings and stronger quadriceps because you mainly use your quadriceps while cycling. You therefore have a muscle imbalance. By incorporating exercises that focus on these imbalances, you'll become stronger and less prone to injury. In this example, you would want to do several exercises that help strengthen your hamstrings to balance out the quadriceps and hamstrings.

Muscle imbalances can also be linear, meaning that you could be stronger with your left arm than with your right. For this reason, you need to incorporate exercises that focus on both the right and left side independently. For example, doing arm curls using a curling bar can prevent a weaker arm from developing as much as the stronger side. By using dumbbells to execute single-arm curls, you are demanding the same response from each arm; neither has the opportunity to assist the other. In the early stages of strength training, you may feel and see this in the number of repetitions you are able to complete with a specific weight. Focus on completing the same number of repetitions with each side using the same weight and speed to develop well-balanced muscle groups. Another benefit of strength training is that building muscle increases metabolism, which helps you burn fat and become leaner.

PREVENT INJURY

When your muscles are balanced and well developed, you are less prone to injuries. By having more muscle fiber and tissue, along with a certain amount of flexibility, you can absorb unforeseen and awkward movements. For example, if you are running and step on a large pine-cone, you may end up rolling your ankle to the outside, causing a twisting movement in your foot and lower leg. A weak and undeveloped lower leg and foot may suffer a sprain, strain, or even a break from this action, whereas a strong and developed lower leg and foot can often absorb the movement and recover with little or no effect on the body. To this end, an athlete who has a well-balanced plan of exercises and sport-specific strength training may rarely be injured, whereas an athlete who does not incorporate strength training into her or his program may be plagued with nagging injuries.

Another item to consider in the development of muscle strength for injury prevention is the incorporation of nonlinear movement into your exercises. Triathlon is a linear sport, meaning that you normally travel straight ahead throughout your training and races. But at times you need to move right or left quickly, such as to avoid a pothole or dodge a rabbit. If you have not developed muscles to support this rapid motion right or left, you could open yourself up to an unforeseen injury caused by your inability to absorb the impact or stress of this rapid nonlinear movement. Modifying a lunge to a side step instead of a forward step is a good example of how to build nonlinear strength and prevent injury.

If you are an older athlete, especially a woman, strength training will help increase your bone density and thus reduce the risk of bone fracture. Sturdy bones are key to staying healthy and strong in your daily activities as well as your triathlon training.

Strength-Training Exercises

All the following exercises can be done in a gym because the gym is likely to have all the equipment, machines, dumbbells, and benches that you need. But you can also do most of these exercises at home by buying a few pieces of equipment. You'll want to invest in a few sets of dumbbells, at least one set of lighter ones and one set of heavier ones. An exercise bench or physioball to do the exercises on and a few stretch cords are also good investments. You can use a couch or your stairs for some of the exercises. You can do many exercises to build strength, and the ones listed can help you get started. You can add more and modify the exercises as you progress in your training. We suggest starting with 2 sets of 10 to 12 repetitions for each exercise. As you get stronger after several weeks, you can increase up to 15 repetitions for each exercise. Or, alternately, increase the weight you use so that 2 sets of 10 to 12 repetitions at a higher weight is still challenging for you.

INCORPORATING STRENGTH TRAINING INTO YOUR BUSY SCHEDULE

You are already spending several hours per week swimming, cycling, and running. Don't become discouraged when we suggest that you add two strength-training sessions of 20 to 30 minutes into your week. To incorporate this activity into your busy schedule, you may need to get creative. Here are some ideas:

Eliminate Wasted Time

To make the most of your time at the gym, on those days when you use the swimming pool or treadmill or take a spinning class, we suggest that you stay an additional 30 minutes afterward to squeeze in a strength-training session or a short treadmill run. That way, you are eliminating the need to drive to the gym every day and can do two workouts in one trip. If the gym you use offers onsite daycare, you can normally leave a child there for up to 90 minutes, which is plenty of time to do back-to-back workouts. Also, if you have kids who attend school, go to daycare, or participate in after-school sports or activities, take advantage of the time when others are watching them or they are doing their own activities to do your own workout. You can do a run near the soccer field or T-ball field and still see what they are doing. You can bring a trainer and your bike to the side of the field and get in a training ride while your child participates in a sport.

If you work in a facility that offers a gym, use your lunch hour to get in a workout. If your workplace has no gym, you can take running clothes to work and run during your lunch break. Many offices now offer at least changing rooms, and some even have showers for active people who like to use their break time to work out.

Take Advantage of Bad Weather or Lack of Daylight

If the weather is bad or if you need to train early in the morning before the sun comes up or in the evening after dark, you can use your time at the gym to your advantage. For example, if you need to run on the treadmill after work because it is storming outside, you can add a 30-minute strength-training session after you run. Your body will already be warmed up from the running, so head over to the weights and knock out a second workout in one trip. If you plan to take a spinning class at the gym, you can add a short treadmill run, swim, or strength-training session afterward to get the most from your time and travel to the gym. You don't always need to go to the gym to do strength training. With a few dumbbells, stretch cords, and creativity, you can do strength training in your living room. You can do several strength-training exercises with no equipment at all, such as squats, lunges, push-ups, step-ups (on your stairs), and triceps push-ups (on your couch). By performing a few sets of these, you can get in a good 20- to 30-minute strength session at home.

Add Equipment to Your Advantage

Incorporate strength training when you're already training for the three main sports. In the pool you can use items like baggy suits, more commonly known as drag suits, or you can use hand paddles to increase resistance while swimming. On the bike, riding hills in a hard gear is a great way to add resistance and build strength while you are riding outside. If you have children, pulling a carriage with your kids in it is a wonderful way to both build strength and spend time with your family. On the run, hills can help build leg strength. Stairs create a great opportunity to build strength during your run. Just as a bike carriage creates resistance on the bike, a jog stroller has long been used by parents who can't leave a child behind during their run. Little do they realize that by adding additional resistance, they are increasing strength and building muscle at the same time.

UPPER-BODY EXERCISES

Upper-body strength exercises are important to include in your triathlon training program because of the muscles you use during swim training. To swim, you use your shoulders, triceps, and back a lot, and by doing our suggested upper-body exercises, you will not only increase and maintain strength but also prevent shoulder injuries. Our favorite upper-body exercises are provided here. While doing these exercises, a general recommendation is two sets of 10 to 12 repetitions.

LAT PULL-DOWN

Purpose

To increase back strength

Description

Position yourself correctly on a lateral pull-down machine. Grab the bar just outside your shoulders or even a little wider. Keep your chest tall, point your elbows straight down, and squeeze your lats. Think of pulling from your armpits as you pull the bar toward you to your chin or just below (see figure *a*). You should keep the bar in front of your body. With control, straighten your arms as the bar rises (see figure *b*).

ASSISTED DIP

Purpose

To increase triceps, shoulder, and chest strength

Description

Position yourself correctly on an assisted dip machine. Stand on the dip bar with your feet shoulder-width apart, your arms straight, and your shoulders above your hands. Step down on the assistance bar, keeping your hips and knees straight. Lower your body until you feel a slight stretch in your shoulders (see figure *a*) and then push your body up until your arms are straight (see figure *b*). With control, lower your body back down to the start position.

ASSISTED PULL-UP

Purpose

To increase biceps, shoulder, and upper-back strength

Description

Position yourself correctly on an assisted pull-up machine. Grip the handles above your shoulders with your palms facing outward. Straighten your arms and step onto the assistance bar so that your body is upright and your abs are engaged. Bend your elbows to lift your body up until your chin is above the height of your hands (see figure *a*). Slowly straighten your elbows to lower to the start position to complete one rep (see figure *b*).

SEATED ROW

Purpose

To increase middle back, biceps, lat, and shoulder strength

Description

You need to use a low pulley machine with a V-grip bar so that your hands can be neutral facing each other. To begin, sit down on the machine and place your feet on the front platform or crossbar, making sure that your knees are slightly bent and not locked. Lean over as you keep the natural alignment of your back and grab the V-bar handles. With your arms extended, pull back until your torso is at a 90-degree angle from your legs (see figure *a*). Your back should be slightly arched and your chest should be lifted. You should feel a good stretch in your lats as you hold the bar in front of you. Keeping your torso stationary, pull the handles back toward your torso while keeping your arms close to your body until you touch your abdominals (see figure *b*). Squeeze your lats, hold the contraction for a second, and slowly return to the start position.

PUSH-UP

Purpose

To increase shoulder, back, triceps, and biceps strength

Description

Lie prone on the floor with the palms of your hands on the floor, slightly wider than shoulder-width apart. Raise your body off the floor by extending your arms with your body straight (see figure *a*). Keeping your body straight, lower your body to the floor by bending your arms (see figure *b*) and repeat.

Modification

You can do these with your knees on the floor if you don't have the strength to do them on your toes.

CHEST PRESS

Purpose

To increase chest and triceps strength

Description

Lie on your back on a flat bench or physio ball with a dumbbell in each hand resting on top of your thighs. With the palms of your hands facing each other, lift the dumbbells so that they are at the sides of your chest. Your upper arm and forearm should create a 90-degree angle. Rotate your wrists so that the palms of your hands are facing away from you (see figure *a*). Maintaining full control of the dumbbells at all times, exhale and use your chest muscles to push the dumbbells up toward the ceiling (see figure *b*). Lock your arms at the top of the lift as you squeeze your chest, hold for a second, and slowly return to the start position.

LATERAL RAISE

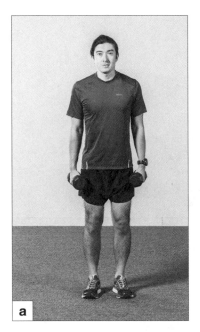

Purpose

To increase shoulder strength

Description

From a standing position with your feet hip-distance apart, hold dumb-bells at your sides with your elbows and knees slightly bent (see figure *a*). Raise the dumbbells to your sides until your elbows are shoulder height (see figure *b*). Lower the dumbbells with control to the start position.

ONE-ARM ROW

Purpose

To increase back, shoulder, and biceps strength

Description

Place your right leg on top of the end of the bench, bend your torso forward from the waist until your upper body is parallel to the floor, and place your right hand on the bench for support. Use your left hand to pick up the dumbbell on the floor and hold the weight while keeping your lower back straight (see figure *a*). The palm of your hand should be facing the bench. Pull the dumbbell straight up to the side of your chest, keeping your upper arm close to your side and your torso stationary (see figure *b*). Only your arm should move; do not try to pull the dumbbell up using your forearms. Lower the dumbbell straight down to the starting position. Repeat on the other side after you complete all repetitions on one side.

TRICEPS KICKBACK

Purpose

To increase triceps strength

Description

Stand to the right of your flat bench and hold a dumbbell in your right hand with your palm facing in. Place your left lower leg and your left hand on top of the bench. Lean forward at the hips until your upper body is parallel to the floor. Bend your right elbow so that your upper arm is parallel to the floor, your forearm is perpendicular to it, and your palm faces in (see figure *a*). Keep your elbow close to your waist. Pull your abdominals in and bend your knees slightly. Keeping your upper arm still, straighten your arm behind you until your entire arm is parallel to the floor and one end of the dumbbell points toward the floor (see figure *b*). Slowly bend your arm to lower the weight. After you complete the set of 10 to 12 repetitions, repeat the exercise with your left arm.

OVERHEAD PRESS

Purpose

To increase shoulder strength

Description

Stand with your feet shoulder-width apart and hold a dumbbell in each hand. Bring the dumbbells up to head height, palms facing forward, with your elbows out and arms at about 90 degrees (see figure *a*). Maintaining strict technique with no leg drive or backward lean, extend through the elbow to raise the weights together directly above your head (see figure *b*). Pause and slowly lower the dumbbells so that your arms are at the 90-degree angle.

LOWER-BODY EXERCISES

Lower-body strength-training exercises are important to include in your training program because of all the muscles you use during cycling and running. You want to maintain good muscle balance in your legs and prevent injuries. We describe here our favorite lower-body exercises.

LEG PRESS

Purpose

To increase quadriceps and glute strength

Description

Position yourself correctly on a leg press machine. Start with your feet about shoulder-width apart in the middle of the platform, parallel to each other. Press the platform with your legs until just before you lock out your knees so that they are almost straight (see figure *a*). Lower the platform back to the point where you have a 90-degree angle in your knees; don't go any farther back than that (see figure *b*). Your feet should stay straight on the platform, not angling out at all.

ALTERNATING LUNGE

Purpose

To increase quadriceps, hamstring, and glute strength and improve balance

Description

Begin standing with feet about hip-distance apart and hands on hips (see figure *a*). Step one leg forward, allowing both knees to bend so that the thigh of the forward leg is parallel to the floor and the knee of the rear leg touches the floor (see figure *b*). Push off with the forward leg to return to the starting position. Repeat with the other leg.

Modifications

Hold onto a chair or bar or decrease your range of motion by not allowing the rear knee to drop all the way to the floor.

SQUAT

Purpose

To increase quadriceps, hamstring, and glute strength

Description

Stand with the chest lifted, look forward, and place your feet shoulder-width apart or slightly wider. Extend your hands straight out in front of you to help keep your balance (see figure *a*). You can also bend your elbows or clasp your fingers. Sit your hips back and down as you bend your knees, as if you're sitting into an imaginary chair. Keep your head facing forward as your upper body hinges forward slightly from the hips. Let your lower back arch slightly as you descend. Lower your hips until your thighs are parallel to the floor, with your knees over your ankles. Press your weight back into your heels (see figure *b*). Keep your body tight and push through your heels to bring yourself back to the starting position. Repeat.

Modification

Decrease your range of motion by stopping before your thighs are parallel to the floor.

STEP-UP

Purpose

To increase quadriceps, hamstring, and glute strength and improve balance

Description

Stand facing the side of a bench or step with your arms at your sides. Place one foot on the bench (see figure *a*). Step up by extending the hip and knee of the first leg and placing your other foot on the bench (see figure *b*). Step down with the second leg by flexing the hip and knee of the first leg. Return to the original standing position by placing the foot of the first leg on the floor. Alternate legs until you complete the desired number of repetitions on both sides.

CORE EXERCISES

Core exercises are important to include in your triathlon strength training because your core is the center of all your training in swimming, cycling, and running. If you have a weak core, you are more prone to injuries, especially to your back. We provide some of our favorite core exercises here.

PLANK

Purpose

To increase abdominal and back strength

Description

Begin in a push-up position on the floor. Bend your elbows 90 degrees and rest your weight on your forearms. Lift your hips off the floor. Your elbows should be directly beneath your shoulders, and your body should form a straight line from your head to your feet (see figure). Hold the position as long as you can. Start with 30 seconds and work your way up to 60 seconds. If necessary, you can modify the exercise by placing your knees on the floor.

PHYSIO BALL CRUNCH

Purpose

To increase abdominal strength

Description

Sit on an exercise ball. Walk forward on the ball so that your back is supported on the ball. Your shoulders and head should be hanging off the ball, and your knees and hips should be bent (see figure *a*). Gently hyperextend your back on the contour of the ball. Place your hands behind your neck and contract your abdominal muscles to raise your upper torso straight up toward the ceiling (see figure *b*). Slowly lower your upper body to the start position.

STRETCHES

Gentle stretching after swimming, cycling, running, or strength training is beneficial. Your muscles should already be warmed up before you stretch; otherwise, you risk injuring yourself. Yoga or Pilates classes can also be beneficial to anyone training for a triathlon. Be careful because intense yoga classes wouldn't necessarily be considered a form of recovery.

Stretching can help keep your muscles from getting sore and is also a good way to relax, meditate, and absorb all the training you are doing. You can spend 5 minutes on a few stretches or up to an hour doing a yoga class. This section provides a few simple stretches that you can do just about anywhere.

HIP STRETCH

Purpose

To keep the hips from getting sore and tight after a lot of cycling and running

Description

Sit on the floor with your left knee bent in front of you. The outer part of your left leg should be lying on the floor so that your left foot is near your right knee. Place the inner part of your right leg on the floor and your right knee out to the side with your right foot behind you. Place your hands on the floor in front of you with your arms straight. Breathe out as you lower your upper body over your front knee until you feel a gentle stretch (see figure). Repeat on the other side.

STANDING QUADRICEPS STRETCH

Purpose

To keep the quadriceps from becoming sore after a lot of cycling and running

Description

Stand tall, holding on to a chair or a wall for balance if you need to. Keep your feet hip-width apart, your back straight, and your feet parallel to each other. Reach back and grab your left foot in your left hand, keeping your thighs lined up next to each other and your left leg in line with your hip (see figure). Hold and repeat on the other side.

STANDING TRICEPS STRETCH

Purpose

To keep the triceps from becoming sore after swimming and strength training

Description

Stand tall and put your left elbow in your right hand. Reach your left arm overhead and place your palm on the center of your back, supporting the elbow in your right hand. Reach your fingertips down your spine, keeping your shoulders relaxed and away from your ears (see figure). Repeat with the other arm.

BACK STRETCH

Purpose

To keep the back open and strong because cycling require a hunched-over position and is hard on the back

Description

Start on your hands and knees with your hands shoulder-width apart and placed under your shoulders, knees hip-width apart and placed directly under your hips, abs engaged, and back flat (spine neutral). Engage your abdominals as if you are pulling your belly button toward your spine and round your back toward the ceiling (see figure). Allow your head and neck to fall naturally between your arms.

NECK STRETCH

Purpose

To keep the neck open and loose and prevent soreness from swimming

Description

You can do this stretch sitting or standing. Tilt your head toward one shoulder and hold for 20 to 30 seconds. For a deeper stretch, gently pull your head toward your shoulder (see figure). Repeat on the other side.

STANDING CALF STRETCH

Purpose

To keep the calves relaxed and prevent soreness from running

Description

Stand and place your hands on a wall in front of you. Place your right foot about 3 feet (90 cm) behind you, making sure that your toes are facing forward. Keep your heel on the ground and lean forward with your right knee straight and left knee bent (see figure). Rotating your toes in and out slightly targets the medial and lateral parts of this muscle separately. Hold for 45 to 60 seconds and repeat on the other side.

We have discussed many topics so far in this book. Strength training and stretching are beneficial to include in your triathlon training program. They will not only help you become stronger, faster, and leaner but also help keep you injury free. In the next chapter, we move into nutrition and rest. These elements are crucial to all the physical training you do to prepare for your triathlon.

CHAPTER 9

NUTRITION AND REST

Proper nutrition and rest are essential but often overlooked components of triathlon training. New triathletes are normally aware of their body's increased need for fuel and fluids during training and competition, but they too often miss the mark on how exactly to fill the void caused by daily training. We discuss how to fuel before, during, and after training for optimal health and performance. Likewise, most new triathletes experience increased fatigue and a desire for rest or sleep with the increased training load. Although it is easy just to say, "Take a nap," we discuss how rest is an essential element of getting stronger and faster and continuing to develop as a triathlete.

Fuel for Triathlon Training

We will be talking in generalities in this chapter. If you are a person who is diabetic or has particular food allergies or other specific dietary needs, we strongly suggest you meet with a Registered Dietician and discuss your particular daily requirements and limitations. Let the dietician know that you are training for a triathlon so that she or he understands your particular added nutritional needs.

DETERMINING YOUR DAILY NUTRITIONAL NEEDS

Let's start by addressing one of the biggest myths in triathlon training. We often hear people say, "I'm in training, so I can basically eat what I want." Although your daily caloric burn will certainly increase based on your training volume, you don't have a license to hit the buffet for every meal. Every person burns calories at a slightly different rate, and every person has a set amount of calories that her or his body requires simply to function each day. Ascertaining these two numbers is the first step in dialing in your nutritional game plan.

The first number we suggest that you determine is your resting metabolic rate (RMR). Your RMR is the base number of calories your body requires during a day with no activity. We look at this number as a baseline. Many online websites offer calculation bots that can give you a basic idea of what your RMR is, but if you have a heart rate monitor, you can calculate it yourself using one of the following formulas:

Males: 9.99 × ___weight (kg) + 6.25 × ___height (cm)
           − 4.92 × ___age (years) + 5

Females: 9.99 × ___weight (kg) + 6.25 × ___height (cm)
           − 4.92 × ___age (years) − 161

Understand that this number is based on an algorithm and may not determine your exact RMR. To determine your exact RMR, you would need to submit to a clinical test. These tests are normally conducted by a trained professional or doctor in a controlled laboratory setting.

The second set of numbers is your caloric burn rate for each of the three sports. Again, these numbers will be unique to your body type, age, and activity. Determining these numbers has recently become simpler because of the proliferation of heart rate monitors and health monitors. If you use these tools correctly, you should be able to determine with reasonable accuracy your total caloric burn for each workout you complete. Typically, a 150-pound (68 kg) person burns about 600 calories per hour running, 500 calories per hour biking, and 450 calories per hour swimming at a consistent aerobic effort. A 200-pound (90 kg) person burns about 760 calories per hour running, 720 calories per hour biking, and 570 calories per hour swimming. So if you weigh 150 pounds, were relatively sedentary for most of the day, and completed a 60-minute aerobic bike ride, your daily caloric requirement would be your RMR plus 500.

Remember that this calculation does not take into account activities such as stair climbing at work or home, running to catch a bus or an elevator, or even lifting groceries or your pet during the day. But it does begin to create an estimate of the calories your body needs to break even. With that knowledge, anything above that number becomes extra and can lead to weight gain over time. Conversely, anything below that number can lead to the reduction of body weight over time. If you plan to lose weight by restricting the number of calories you consume, you should set a goal of running a relatively small deficit of calories (less than 500) per day so that you don't starve yourself and negatively affect your body's ability to recover.

TIMING YOUR NUTRITION

Now that you better understand how many calories your body needs during a day, you should know when to take in calories during the day and in what form.

Fueling Throughout the Day

When it comes to fueling during your triathlon training, not all calories are the same. For instance, the number of calories in a banana may be equal to that in a mixed alcohol drink, but we would never recommend refueling with a cocktail after a workout. Consuming quality calories from real foods low in saturated fat and simple sugars is an ideal way to fuel and refuel your body. The body processes such foods more efficiently, and they normally hold a higher nutritional value and contain numerous vitamins and minerals that are essential for maintaining a healthy body. Although processed or man-made foods and supplements can be substituted during some meals, we recommend keeping those items to a minimum in your daily food consumption. We will address sports drinks and sports nutrition items such as gels, blocks, and bars later.

As a triathlete, you need to understand how the food you eat is burned and converted to fuel or energy. Carbohydrate is a main source of energy in a triathlete's diet, but as with other nutrients, the various forms of carbohydrate are not equal in how they fuel the body. All foods are assigned a number between 1 and 100 on the glycemic index (GI). The GI is essentially a way to rate how fast the body burns the food we eat as fuel. For example, white bread is assigned a relatively high number on the GI, meaning that it is turned into energy quickly and does not supply a long-lasting source of fuel. On the other hand, whole-grain bread is generally assigned a lower number on the GI, meaning that it is not digested quickly and therefore provides a slower-acting, longer-lasting source of fuel. Foods with a higher GI rating increase blood sugar level faster than those with a lower GI rating. For meals, we recommend focusing on consuming lower GI carbohydrate to provide longer-lasting fuel sources. During longer training sessions or during your event, fuel sources with a high GI index are more acceptable because you may be requiring quick and simple sources of calories. Sports gels, blocks, and bars come into play here. These items are normally high in simple sugars and provide a quick boost of energy that normally lasts less than 45 minutes. Because these products are normally high in sugar, you should consume them with 4 to 6 ounces (120 to 180 ml) of water. Consuming them with sports drinks that are high in sugar can lead to an upset stomach or gastrointestinal distress.

Here are a few common low GI foods:

Milk

Yogurt

Oatmeal

Fresh fruit (oranges, grapefruits, plums, apples, pears, peaches, dried fruit)

Granola

Bars (made with whole grains, dried fruit, and little added sugar)

Whole-grain toast

Beans

Brown rice

Lentils

Peanuts

Cashews

During training, we recommend taking the approach of consistently fueling yourself throughout the day by consuming a series of smaller balanced meals versus a few larger meals. By consuming five smaller meals consisting of lean protein, low GI carbohydrate, fruits, and vegetables, you not only create a more consistent fueling platform for your body but also are able to insert workouts into your day without having to deal with a full stomach. Eating smaller, more consistent meals also helps keep your blood sugar levels in a more consistent range, which will help prevent the afternoon drowsiness that can come after eating a large lunch. See table 9.1 for sample daily menus that will keep your blood sugar level consistent and your energy up for your training.

In addition, hydrating yourself consistently in this format is just as beneficial. Instead of consuming large amounts of water at one or two times during the day, you can hydrate your body more effectively by sipping small amounts of water throughout the day. Keeping a water bottle close to you at all times will assist in this process, especially if you work at a desk or other location where water is not readily available or convenient to grab often.

Fueling Before and After a Workout

Fueling before and refueling after workouts is another important aspect of training that should not be taken lightly. If you have a habit of working out first thing in the morning before breakfast, you should consume a small amount of calories (150 to 250 calories) and water about 30 minutes before starting your workout. Because you were most likely sleeping for 5 to 7 hours before waking up and probably have not eaten in the past 7 to 9 hours, your body needs a little fuel to get it moving. Going into an early workout starving prevents your body from performing as it should. Moreover, the thought of being hungry can divert your concentration from your workout and technique performance. Some examples of a good snack are the following:

A handful of dry cereal and 6 ounces (180 ml) of water

1 tablespoon of peanut butter

A banana or an apple

An energy bar

Small protein smoothie

Table 9.1 Sample Menus for Typical Triathlon Training Day

	Sample menu 1	Sample menu 2	Sample menu 3	Sample menu 4
Meal 1: breakfast	Oatmeal with a banana, almond slices, and coffee	Smoothie with protein, fruit, and soy milk	Two eggs with toast, fruit, and coffee	Steel-cut oats, blueberries, and coffee
Meal 2: mid-morning snack	Greek yogurt with a scoop of granola	Handful of pistachios and a piece of fruit	Cottage cheese and fresh peach slices	Almond butter and strawberries on a rice cake
Meal 3: lunch	Salad with veggies, lean protein, an apple, and cheese	Turkey wrap with veggies, fruit	Peanut butter and jelly sandwich on whole grain, fresh fruit, and sugar snap peas	Black beans, rice, carnitas, lettuce and veggie bowl
Meal 4: afternoon snack	Fresh fruit with 2 tablespoons of peanut or almond butter	Veggies with hummus	1/2 cup of trail mix with almonds, sesame seeds, dried fruit, and chocolate chips	Whole-grain crackers with cheese
Meal 5: dinner	Lean protein such as chicken, fish, or tofu; veggies; and quinoa	Lean protein, grilled veggies, and fruit salad	Chicken or lean steak and veggie kabobs, grilled zucchini, and couscous salad	Grilled salmon, asparagus, and a side salad

After you finish your workout, try to eat a meal within 30 to 60 minutes. Your body needs to refuel so that it can continue to give you energy for the rest of the day. How you refuel should be consistent with the intensity and duration of the workout you just completed. If you complete an easy 30-minute bike ride, your calorie refueling needs will not be the same as when you complete a 60-minute aerobic run. Use the information about burning calories we spoke of earlier to determine how many calories you need to consume after your workout.

Note here that at times you may find yourself having to squeeze in a workout between previous commitments, therefore not allowing you to eat a solid meal. In these instances, having meal replacement bars and bottled water can buy you some time until you can get to a good meal. These items can be safely stored in desks, cars, or gym bags. A processed food product would be a good choice in these circumstances. A poor choice would be not to eat at all and simply wait until you can get to a meal. Starving yourself in this fashion can lead to overeating, unwanted snacking, or fatigue. When looking for the right bar, the product with the least processing and lowest level of sugar is the best choice. Bars with nuts, honey, sea salt, brown rice cereal, agave nectar, and chocolate chips are good. Many of the bars with ingredients that are more natural have 190 to 225 calories, 8 to 17 grams of fat, and 5 to 7 grams of protein.

Fueling During a Workout

The goal of eating and drinking during your workouts and racing is to replenish calories burned and hydration lost. If your workout lasts less than 90 minutes, you will likely not need to eat anything. Simply hydrating with water should be sufficient. During your training and racing you typically tap into one of two energy sources in your body. You draw energy either from glycogen stores or from fat stores. The human body typically has about 3,000 calories of energy stored as glycogen and 80,000 calories of energy stored as fat. You draw from these two reservoirs at different times. When you are exerting energy at or above your aerobic threshold, your body uses glycogen as energy. It can convert glycogen to energy fairly quickly, but it also uses this fuel fairly quickly. You can replenish glycogen calories with gels and blocks because, as we said earlier, these items are normally made of simple sugar. Be aware that gels and blocks normally offer only 75 to 100 calories and can be taken only about every 45 to 60 minutes. So if you're burning 1,000 calories per hour and can replenish only 100 of those per hour, you can see that glycogen is not a sustainable source of fuel for the long term. Fat calories, on the other hand, are burned much more slowly and are available from a vast reservoir of fuel. Fat calories are not as quickly accessed, and converting them to energy takes longer. Fat calories are not a source of fuel you will try to replenish during a workout or event. Your body uses fat calories as a fuel source when it is operating below your aerobic threshold. For that reason and others, you can go longer during a workout at an easier pace.

Throughout this entire process of working out or racing, your body is using water either to help covert calories to energy or to cool the skin by creating sweat. Water is a vital element of your body, and for that reason we prefer it as a rehydration product to sports drinks, which normally contain unwanted sugar. Water can serve other purposes as well; you can use it to rinse sticky hands, to splash your face, or to cool your head or back. The trick to staying properly hydrated is to take small sips often, about every 2 1/2 to 5 minutes. By taking small sips, you allow your stomach to process what you have consumed and you are less likely to create that bloated, upset feeling in your gut. Knowing whether you are properly hydrated during your day is an easy task. When you urinate, note the color and smell. We know that this method may seem gross, but trust us here. Dark yellow and pungent urine is a good indicator you are dehydrated and should drink more water. Going all day without urinating is another sign you are likely dehydrated. If your urine is clear with no smell, you may be overhydrated, which can lead to the leaching of nutrients and minerals from your body. Ideally, you want your urine to be a very light yellow, and you should have the urge to urinate about once every 1 to 2 hours.

Other dietary trends or needs can affect how you consume calories and offer unique challenges to triathlon training. Trends like the paleo diet limit your caloric options and can prevent you from consuming the correct balance of nutrients and minerals required for training. Sure, most cavemen and cavewomen were skinny, but they were not swimming, biking, and running as a hobby. We suggest that you bypass trends such as these and focus on eating correct portions of real foods. Those who have food allergies or social issues with certain foods may find it beneficial to meet with a dictician. Vegetarians and vegans need to find appropriate ways to consume higher levels of protein and iron during training. These two essential elements in the bloodstream become building blocks to creating lean muscle.

Fueling for Race Day

"How do I fuel on race day?" is a question many athletes ask. You don't want to go into a race with too much food in your stomach. If you do, you could end up with terrible GI distress. You also don't want to go into a race underfueled and not have enough energy to complete the race. So how do you find the balance between too much and too little (which can result in what is known as bonking)? Let's discuss race-day fueling.

Assuming that your event is a morning race, your dinner the night before should be simple and at a reasonable time, say 6:30 p.m. This dinner should not be a "carbo load"; it should be a typical well-balanced meal. This is not the time to experiment, so it's wise to avoid anything new to your diet. Nothing is worse than waking up race morning with a stomachache. We also recommend you avoid red meat because it can be hard to digest and can lead to an unsettled and upset stomach on race morning. Chicken and pasta are always good go-to foods, or, if you are traveling, pizza can offer consistency that is relatively balanced in both carbohydrate and protein (just don't eat the whole thing!).

On race morning, eat your breakfast about 3 hours before the start of your event to allow optimal digestion of your food and ideally produce a bowel movement. In terms of foods, stick with the basics; bananas, oatmeal, bagels, waffles, juice, and coffee are all good options. We suggest you avoid dairy products because they can cause stomach distress. An hour before your event, you can snack on an energy bar and sip on some water to help you stay topped off in the nutrition and hydration department.

You should practice your prerace meal a few times during training. Wake up a little early on a weekend and pretend it is race day. Eat what you think you might on race morning, do your workout, and afterward evaluate how your meal affected your performance. If it worked well, great. Lock it down. If it did not feel right, try again next week. Never wake up race morning and try something new. We never do anything new on race day.

Fueling After a Race

Proper refueling and hydration after your race is key to your recovery process. Drink plenty of water to rehydrate your body. You should also try to get in some sort of nutrition within the 30 minutes after the race. If you have a queasy stomach, try some water first. Then, about 25 minutes postrace, see whether you can tolerate a banana or apple with peanut butter or some crackers with cheese. You don't need to eat a lot of food; even 100 to 150 calories will help. Within 1 to 3 hours after your race, assuming that your stomach has settled down, you can eat a small meal or snack with carbohydrate and protein. You don't want to eat more than necessary, but you want to refuel for recovery. Here are a few examples:

   Sweet potato

   Protein shake

   Protein bar

   Grilled chicken and avocado salad

   Veggie omelet and fruit

   Steak salad

What you eat after a race is more important than some people realize.

Posttraining Rest

Now that you have fueled, worked out, and refueled, you need to incorporate some rest. Muscle adaption and development comes through a process of stressing the muscle fibers through exercise and then allowing them to recover through rest.

INCORPORATING REST THROUGH PERIODIZATION

You will see in the training programs later in this book that we incorporate rest in the beginning of each week and then on the fourth week of every 4-week cycle. We incorporate rest early in the week because your training volume and intensity is usually at its peak during the weekend when you have time to train. Because you have taxed your body on the weekend, you need to let it recover so that you can do it all over again. If you do not get adequate rest, the muscles will fatigue and eventually fail, resulting in injury.

Along that same thought process, we progressively build up your training volume and intensity over a 3-week period leading to lower intensity and volume for the fourth week. This approach, known as periodization, is the basis of most sports training programs. Periodization is the art of balancing a progressively increasing training load with

---

RUNNING IN YOUR AEROBIC ZONE

One of the hardest things for people to do is to run easy. A trick to enable you to run in an easy aerobic zone is to run while breathing only through your nose. By not allowing yourself to breathe through your mouth, you limit the amount of oxygen you can take in, which in turn limits your effort level. If you find yourself needing to breathe through your mouth, slow down. In the beginning you may only be able to manage a fast walk, but over time as you develop your cardiopulmonary system, you will be able to run easy while breathing only through your nose. You can also choose to run with someone who is slightly slower than you are to keep your pace consistently in your aerobic zone. Or, if you own a heart rate monitor or an activity counter that has heart rate monitoring, you can check your heart rate while running. Running in your aerobic zone can aid your recovery and keep you strong and injury free for all the other training you are doing for the swim, bike, and run. Building your running aerobic endurance enhances your endurance in swimming and cycling as well.

adequate rest and recovery to produce consistent training gains. Rest can come in several forms. The most common two are a day off from training, as shocking as that may be, and active recovery. Active recovery is a way to keep the body moving while not taxing its energy stores. This can come in the form of an easy swim, bike, or run; Pilates; or an easy yoga class.

KNOWING WHEN YOUR BODY NEEDS REST

During your training you need to listen to your body. If you start to develop small wandering pains or aches, your body telling may be telling you to slow down a bit. One of the best ways to read your body is to use your waking heart rate. This practice is easy, but you may need a few days to perfect it. Start by placing a clock next to your bed at night. When you wake up the next morning, do not move except to bring one of your hands slowly to your wrist or neck. Take your pulse and record the number. Over the next couple of days, you should notice a trend. Your waking heart rate is an excellent early indicator of overtraining and illness. If your waking heart rate exceeds 7 to 10 beats above normal, you should think strongly about taking that day off from training or backing down the intensity to an easy level. The reasoning is that if your heart rate is elevated when you are sleeping, your body is working hard to repair something. This method has worked for athletes over the years in many sports.

Several products on the market can monitor your sleep quality. These data can indicate whether you are coming down with something or have just been working too hard. Your goal is to sleep a minimum of 7 to 9 hours per night. Avoiding injury is a key skill that most triathletes need to practice. If you find yourself getting sick, do not make the common mistake of making up the workout after you feel better. By stacking workouts, you overload your training plan and risk future injury. Waking up unrested and overtired to do an early morning workout might be a sign that you are pushing it. You may need to choose an extra hour of sleep that day instead of training. The same goes for a lunch workout or after-work or evening workout. Listen to your body. If it is telling you that it's exhausted and feels a little off, opt for rest or a supereasy workout rather than an intense hard one. One thing we like to tell athletes is to go ahead and start a workout. If they aren't feeling better 15 minutes into it, they should stop, go home, rest, and recover. Occasionally, your body just needs more rest, and you shouldn't stress about it. You should forget about missed workouts because of extreme fatigue; you surely don't want to end up sick or injured because you pushed your body too far. Rest is a vital part of your triathlon training plan.

TAPERING BEFORE A RACE

Tapering is also part of periodization. A taper is a gradual decrease in volume and intensity to allow optimal race performance. A taper for a sprint triathlon should last anywhere from 7 to 14 days depending on the fitness of the athlete. Lesser-trained athletes will benefit more from a longer taper because they need a more gradual acclimation to lower intensity and volume. A taper is meant to deliver the athlete both fresh and ready on race day. No hard and fast rules apply here. Each athlete may experience a different result, but as a rule of thumb, the more trained an athlete is, the less taper is needed.

The following are sample weeklong tapers for each level of athlete—bronze, silver, and gold.

Sample Sprint-Distance Taper Week for a Bronze-Level Athlete

Monday—3-mile (4.8 km) run

Tuesday—15-mile (24 km) bike ride

Wednesday—1,000-meter swim

Thursday—3-mile (4.8 km) run and 800-meter swim or less

Friday—Off

Saturday—1.5-mile (2.4 km) run and 18-minute bike ride (to wake up the legs before the race)

Sunday—Race day

Sample Sprint-Distance Taper Week for a Silver-Level Athlete

Monday—3-mile (5 km) run

Tuesday—20-mile (32 km) bike ride and 600-meter swim

Wednesday—Off or easy 10-mile (16 km) bike ride

Thursday—800-meter swim

Friday—Off

Saturday—1.5-mile (2.4 km) run and 20-minute bike ride (to wake up the legs before the race)

Sunday—Race day

Sample Sprint-Distance Taper Week for a Gold-Level Athlete

Monday—4-mile (6.4 km) run

Tuesday—20-mile (32 km) bike ride and 1,200-meter swim

Wednesday—2-mile (3.2 km) run and easy 10-mile (16 km) bike ride

Thursday—1,000-meter swim

Friday—Off

Saturday—2-mile (3.2 km) run and 30-minute bike ride (to wake up the legs before the race)

Sunday—Race day

Tapers are often executed incorrectly. From the starting point of the taper, the training program begins to decrease progressively in volume and intensity, but many people either train hard too close to their race, thinking they need one last hard workout, or they simply take a week or a few days off before a race as their taper. Both approaches are incorrect. The panic workout will only hurt the athlete because it occurs too close to the race for it to provide any training benefit. The body needs approximately 2 weeks to process the stress of a hard workout and convert it into peak racing energy. An athlete who rests too much or too close to an event risks coming in flat, that is, feeling sluggish and slow. The best approach to race day is to rest 2 days before the event and then do a quick workout in all three sports the day before, lasting no more than 45 minutes total. This shakeout workout freshens up the legs and keeps you peppy for your race.

———————————

Just because you are a triathlete in training, you don't get a hall pass to eat anything you want whenever you want. In fact, you now have to keep a close check on what is going into your mouth and when. By balancing your eating with proper hydration and rest habits, you will draw closer to your goal of becoming a true triathlete. In the next chapter we discuss sprint training plans for bronze-, silver-, and gold-level athletes.

CHAPTER 10

SPRINT-DISTANCE TRIATHLON TRAINING PLANS

We've talked in the previous chapters about swimming, cycling, running, strength training, gear selection, nutrition, rest, and much more for your first triathlon. Now we put it all together and discuss training plans for bronze-, silver-, and gold-level triathletes. These plans are based on the assumption you have read the previous nine chapters, taken the Triathlon Readiness Assessment, and do not have injuries or other conditions that would prevent you from safely performing the training prescribed.

For most of you reading this book, we suggest you start with a sprint-distance race as your first race. A sprint-distance race typically consists of a 750-meter swim, a 20-kilometer bike, and a 5-kilometer run.

Sprint-Distance Plan Basics

Here we discuss the basic information you can expect from the sprint-distance training plans. This material includes where you might be training; the warm-up, main set, and cool-down; and the pace for your swim, bike, and run.

- *Swim*: You will likely swim in a 25-meter or 25-yard pool. Follow the plan and swim yards or meters; it doesn't matter which. Each plan consists of a warm-up, main set, and cool-down. Ideally, you will find a place to swim in the open water a few times before race day so that you become familiar with swimming in a straight line without following a line at the bottom of the pool. The swim workouts are given in distance as well as goal pace. If you can't reach that pace, don't worry; you can adjust those paces as needed.

- *Bike*: Some of the bike workouts are prescribed for outdoors; others are prescribed for the trainer. The bike workouts are given in time with a warm-up, main set, and cool-down. Specific drills, hills, and sprints are also listed.

- *Run*: The running workouts are prescribed in time and effort at certain paces. Some of the workouts are for the treadmill, using the incline for hills, and others are for outside. Your situation and schedule will determine when you choose to run outdoors versus indoors.

Training for a sprint-distance triathlon should start 8 weeks before the race date. You will gradually increase how often you train (frequency), how long each training session is (duration), and how hard each workout is (intensity) as you move into the weeks closest to race day.

- A bronze-level athlete (beginner in all three sports) should train between 5 and 7 hours per week and have a day completely off each week.

- A silver-level athlete (intermediate in all three sports) should train between 6 and 8 hours per week and have either a day completely off or a very easy day once per week.

- A gold-level athlete (advanced in all three sports) should train between 7 and 9 hours per week and have either a day completely off or a very easy day once per week.

For the days when two workouts are prescribed, you should keep at least 3 to 4 hours between the swim, bike, and run workouts, unless a brick workout (back-to-back sessions) is prescribed. You can do a strength session following any of the swim, bike, and run workouts prescribed for that day to save time. Or you can split up the day and do your swim, bike, or run in the morning and strength training in the evening.

You may want to customize these plans further. For example, if you are a bronze-level swimmer but a silver-level runner, you can replace the run segment of the bronze plan with the silver plan.

In addition, although the plans in this chapter specify the days of the week to perform each workout and space out the workouts to allow adequate rest and recovery, the plan is flexible and can be modified to meet your scheduling needs. For example, if you need to move the swim workouts from Tuesday, Thursday, and Saturday to Wednesday, Friday, and Sunday, you can do so. You would then just switch the bike and run workout days as well. Above all, note that the training plans are flexible in that you can do them at the time of day and on the days of the week that work best for you.

Sample Sprint-Distance Triathlon Plans

We offer sample 8-week sprint-distance triathlon plans for bronze-level, silver-level, and gold-level athletes. The training plans include the swim, bike, run, and strength-training workouts as well as any rest or recovery days. We work with a 7-day week cycle and place the workouts within those weeks on the ideal day for you to complete them. For example, we space out the run workouts on alternating days so that you aren't running 3 days in a row. We realize, however, that you may need to rearrange these workouts to meet your scheduling needs. We have put in a few optional strength-training workouts for you to use if you have extra time or happen to find yourself at home unable to get in a swim, bike, or run workout. That way, you can always do functional strength training to get in a workout on that day.

Note that the following workouts are written using a type of short-hand. The more you swim, the more accustomed you will become to interpreting it. For example, 3 × 100 FR @ 2:40 is read "3 by 100 free on the 2:40." This means that you do three repetitions of 100 yards (m) in which each 100-yard swim, along with a small bit of rest, should occur within 2 minutes and 40 seconds. Should you not be able to swim the 100 yards and have at least 10 seconds of rest inside the 2:40, feel free to stretch out these times a bit further. Each interval is designed to have a bit of rest. Also, when the table reads "3 times" that means to repeat what is below it that number of times. A key of the shorthand can be found on the part III opener. There are three drills that appear in these tables that are not described in the chapters of this book. The descriptions for those drills are below.

[1]Catch-up drill: This drill focuses on timing. As one hand enters the water and extends forward, it remains in this position until the opposite hand enters and touches the original hand. At that moment the original hand begins a catch, pull, recovery, and entry then touching the opposite hand signaling its turn to catch, pull, exit, recovery, and enter again. Using a swim aid such as a kick board can help with the hand switching. The kick board will remain in front of you while you essentially pass it back and forth between lead hands. The use of fins or a pull buoy during this drill can help with extra buoyancy.

[2]Single-arm drill: This drill allows you to focus on one side of the body at a time. Begin with extending your nonbreathing-side hand straight forward, then execute a normal swim stroke and breathing pattern with the single arm. For example if you are breathing on your right side, your left hand is stretched out and does not move as your right hand executes a normal swim stroke cycle. Switch hands and breathing sides every length. The use of fins or a pull buoy during this drill can help with extra buoyancy.

[3]Triple switch drill: This drill is similar to the single-arm drill, where you will make three swim stroke cycles with your right hand, take three normal two-handed swim stroke cycles, then three swim stroke cycles with only your left hand while your right hand is stretched out forward, back to three, two-handed normal swim stroke cycles, then three single-arm stroke cycles with your right hand only. Repeat this pattern for the entire swim length.

Bronze-Level Sprint-Distance Triathlon Training Plan

WEEK 1

	Swim	Bike	Run	Strength training
Monday	Off	Off	Off	Off
Tuesday	1 × 200 CH 1 × 400 FR @ 10:00 (2:30) 6 × 50 CH @ 1:20 1 × 300 FR @ 7:00 (2:20) 4 × 50 CH @ 1:15 1 × 200 FR @ 4:30 (2:15) 2 × 50 CH @ 1:10 1 × 100 FR @ 2:10 50 EZ **Total: 1,850**		30 min aerobic pace	
Wednesday		10 min warm-up at easy aerobic pace; 3 × 10 sec seated sprint, 20 sec recovery spin at easy aerobic pace; then repeat the following for 45 min: seated sprint for 20 sec, recovery spin at easy aerobic pace for 40 sec, seated sprint for 30 sec, and recovery spin at easy aerobic pace for 60 sec		20 min strength training (optional)
Thursday	1 × 200 CH 2 × 150 K-DR-S @ 4:30 2 × 150 DR-S @ 4:20 2 × 150 CH @ 4:10 2 × 150 FR @ 4:00 1 × 500 FR @ 12:15 (2:15) 50 EZ **Total: 1,950**			

	Swim	Bike	Run	Strength training
Friday		45 min trainer session: 10 min skill warm-up on trainer (3 × 1 min standing big gear, 1 min seated fast spin at >100 cadence, and 1 min single-leg circular pedaling); 3 × 3 min strong aerobic pace on trainer; 2 min easy aerobic pace between; and 11 min cool-down at light resistance and high cadence	4 × 2 min at 80% aerobic effort and 2 min easy aerobic pace between for 35 min —or— 5 min aerobic run with 1 min walk between and repeat for 35 min	
Saturday	1 × 100 FR 1 × 100 CH 3 × 50 CH @ 1:30 3 times 1 × 200 F @ 4:00 2 × 50 EZ-CH @ 2:00 3 × 50 CH @ 2:00 3 times 1 × 200 F @ 4:00 2 × 50 EZ-CH @ 2:00 **Total: 2,300**			30 min strength training (optional)
Sunday		Aerobic pace on outdoor hills as efficiently as possible and mostly seated and controlled (simulated if inside) for 60 min	6 min aerobic run with 2 min walk between and repeat for 35 min	

Bronze-Level Sprint-Distance Triathlon Training Plan

WEEK 2

	Swim	Bike	Run	Strength training
Monday	Off	Off	Off	Off
Tuesday		Easy aerobic pace for 30 min	4 × 1 min strong aerobic pace at high cadence and 1 min easy aerobic pace between for 35 min	
Wednesday	1 × 200 CH 2 times 1 × 100 FR @ 2:30 1 × 150 NF @ 4:15 200 FR @ 4:30 5 × 50 CH @ 1:10 (odd—F; even—EZ) 3 × 50 K @ 1:45 50 EZ **Total: 2,000**			20 min strength training (optional)
Thursday		4 × 20 sec aerobic sprint with 40 sec rest between; 2 × 5 min strong aerobic (build to strong aerobic by 2 min) with 3 min easy aerobic between for 60 min	6 × 30 sec hill repeats with good form at aerobic pace for 50 min—not a superhard effort, just jogging pace	
Friday	1 × 200 FR 1 × 100 CH 2 times 1 × 50 K @ 1:40 1 × 100 CH @ 2:40 3 × 150 FR @ 3:40 descending 1 × 100 CH @ 2:40 1 × 50 RB-DPS @ 1:40 50 EZ **Total: 1,850**			30 min strength training (optional)
Saturday			Aerobic pace for 40 min	
Sunday	100 FR 100 CH 3 × 50 CH @ 1:30 3 times 1 × 200 F @ 4:00 2 × 50 EZ-CH @ 2:00 3 × 50 CH @ 2:00 3 times 1 × 200 F @ 4:00 2 × 50 EZ-CH @ 2:00 **Total: 2,300**	3 × (1 min single leg, 1 min fast spin, 1 min standing) aerobic pace and 2 min easy aerobic between for 70 min		

Bronze-Level Sprint-Distance Triathlon Training Plan
WEEK 3

	Swim	Bike	Run	Strength training
Monday	Off	Off	Off	Off
Tuesday	200 FR 100 CH 3 × 100 K-S @ 2:30 2 times 1 × 200 FR @ 4:45 1 × 150 FR @ 3:30 1 × 100 FR @ 2:15 50 EZ 3 × 100 K @ 2:45 50 EZ **Total: 1,950**		Easy aerobic pace for 30 min if you feel rested enough, otherwise skip	
Wednesday		Aerobic pace on trainer with 3 × 3 min strong aerobic pace for the last 30 min and 5 min threshold pace between for 45 min		20 min strength training
Thursday	200 FR 150 NF 100 CH 2 times 2 × 50 K @ 1:30 1 × 100 CH-NF @ 2:20 2 × 100 F @ 2:30 1 × 100 CH @ 2:20 2 × 50 DR-S @ 1:30 50 EZ **Total: 1,750**		4 × 90 sec on treadmill at aerobic pace with 2–3% incline and 3 min easy aerobic pace between for 30 min	
Friday		Easy aerobic pace with cadence at 90 RPM for 60 min		
Saturday	200 CH 2 × 50 K-DR @ 2:00 2 times 3 × 100 FR @ 2:40 2 × 50 CH @ 1:30 2 × 100 FR @ 2:20 1 × 50 CH @ 1:40 1 × 100 FR @ 2:00 50 EZ **Total: 1,900**	10 min aerobic warm-up and 20 min strong aerobic pace with 10 min aerobic between for 60 min	3 × 5 min at 75–80% aerobic effort and 5 min easy aerobic pace between for 45 min	
Sunday		Easy aerobic cool-down ride for 30 min		30 min strength training

Bronze-Level Sprint-Distance Triathlon Training Plan
WEEK 4

	Swim	Bike	Run	Strength training
Monday	Off	Off	Off	Off
Tuesday	100 FR 100 CH 3 × 100 CH @ 2:25 3 × 100 FR @ 2:20, 2:15, 2:10 3 × 100 CH @ 2:30 2 × 150 FR 3:30, 3:15 3 × 100 CH @ 2:35 1 × 200 FR @ 4:00 50 EZ **Total: 1,950**	10 min warm-up at easy aerobic pace; 3 × 10 sec seated sprint; 20 sec recovery spin at easy aerobic pace; then repeat the following for 40 min: seated sprint for 20 sec, recovery spin at easy aerobic pace for 40 sec, seated sprint for 30 sec, and recovery spin at easy aerobic pace for 60 sec	Aerobic pace for 35 min	
Wednesday	Off	Off	Off	Off
Thursday	200 CH 1 × 300 FR @ 6:45 (2:15) 2 × 200 FR @ 4:25 (2:12) 3 × 150 FR @ 3:15 (2:10) 3 × 100 FR @ 2:05 4 × 50 FR @ 1:45 50 EZ **Total: 1,900**	60 min trainer session: 20 min skill warm-up on trainer (5 × 1 min standing big gear, 1 min seated fast spin at 100+ cadence); 2 × 5 min at strong aerobic pace with 5 min aerobic pace between; and 15 min light-resistance, high-cadence cool-down	Aerobic pace with last 5 min at 85% effort for 45 min	
Friday	Off	Off	Off	Off

Saturday	100 FR
	100 CH
	3 times
	50 K @ 1:30
	50 DR @ 1:25
	50 CH @ 1:20
	3 × 200 FR @ 4:30
	  descending
	3 times
	50 SC @ 1:30
	50 NF @ 1:20
	50 FR @ 1:10
	3 × 100 FR @ 2:15
	  descending
	50 EZ
	Total: 2,050
			8 min run at aerobic pace with 2 min walk between for 60 min	

Sunday		5 × 3 min (seated and controlled, bigger gear) at aerobic pace for 70 min	Easy aerobic pace for 30 min	

Bronze-Level Sprint-Distance Triathlon Training Plan
WEEK 5

	Swim	Bike	Run	Strength training
Monday	Off	Off	Off	Off
Tuesday		Easy aerobic pace for 30 min	Easy aerobic pace for 30 min	
Wednesday	200 FR 150 NF 100 CH 5 × 50 DR @ 1:30 (odd—fingertip drag; even—catch-up[1]) 4 × 50 SC-K @ 1:40 3 × 50 DPS-RB @ 1:20 2 × 200 FR @ 5:30 descending 50 EZ **Total: 1,700**		6 × 20 sec strides at aerobic pace at 90% effort and 40 sec easy aerobic pace between for 45 min	
Thursday		4 × 20 sec sprint at aerobic pace with 40 sec rest between; 3 × 5 min builds (aerobic to strong aerobic for the last 3 min) with 2 min rest between for 45 min		30 min strength training
Friday	200 CH 4 × 75 CH @ 1:45 2 times 1 × 50 K @ 1:30 2 × 50 CH @ 1:20 3 × 50 CH @ 1:10 1 × 250 FR @ 4:45 50 EZ 4 × 75 DPS-RB @ 1:45 50 EZ **Total: 2,050**		Easy aerobic pace for 20 min	
Saturday		3 × (1 min single leg, 1 min fast spin, 1 min standing) aerobic pace with 2 min easy aerobic between for 30 min	Aerobic pace on a hilly course (uphill at 85–90% effort and easy aerobic recovery on the downhill) for 60 min	
Sunday	200 CH 3 × 100 K-SC-DR-S @ 1:50 3 times 2 × 50 BLD @ 1:10 1 × 100 CH @ 2:20 2 × 50 F @ 1:05 1 × 150 DPS @ 3:30 4 × 50 K @ 1:30 50 EZ **Total: 2,000**	Easy aerobic pace outside for 60 min		

Bronze-Level Sprint-Distance Triathlon Training Plan
WEEK 6

	Swim	Bike	Run	Strength training
Monday		Aerobic pace on trainer with 3 × 4 min strong aerobic pace for the last 30 min and 5 min threshold pace between for 60 min		
Tuesday	200 FR 100 CH 3 × 100 K @ 2:30/2:40 2 × 200 CH @ 4:05/4:30 2 × 100 K @ 2:20/2:30 2 × 150 CH @ 2:55/3:20 1 × 100 K @ 2:20/2:20 2 × 100 CH @ 2:05/2:15 50 EZ **Total: 1,850**		5 × 10 sec strides at aerobic pace with 20 sec easy aerobic pace between for 30 min	
Wednesday		Easy aerobic pace with cadence at 90 for 30 min		30 min strength training
Thursday	200 FR 100 CH 2 times 1 × 150 FR @ 3:05 (3:20) 2 × 125 FR @ 2:45 (3:00) 2 × 100 CH @ 2:25 (2:40) 3 × 50 DR @ 1:20 (1:25) 4 × 25 SC @ :45 (:45) **Total: 2,000**		Walk or jog at aerobic pace with 10 min at 3–4% incline for 40 min	
Friday		Aerobic pace for 20 min and 10 min strong aerobic pace with 10 min aerobic pace between for 80 min		
Saturday	200 CH 2 times 2 × 50 K @ 1:30 (1:35) 2 × 100 FR @ 2:15 (2:25) 1 × 250 FR @ 5:20 (5:45) 2 × 100 NF @ 2:30 (2:40) 2 × 50 SC-DR @ 1:30 (1:35) **Total: 1,900**		Aerobic pace for 45 min	
Sunday		3 × 4 min aerobic pace and strong aerobic for the last 30 min with 5 min threshold pace between for 60 min		20 min strength training

Bronze-Level Sprint-Distance Triathlon Training Plan
WEEK 7

	Swim	Bike	Run	Strength training
Monday		3 × 10, 20, 30 sec seated sprints at easy aerobic pace with 20, 40, and 60 sec easy aerobic spin between for 60 min		
Tuesday	200 FR 100 K 100 NF 8 × 25 DR @ :40 (two different types of drills, one on the even intervals and the other on the odd intervals) 3 × 100 FR @ 2:15 4 times 1 × 125 CH @ 2:50 1 × 75 K-CH @ 2:00 (25 K, 50 CH) 1 × 50 FR-NF @ 1:25 (alternate FR and NF each round) 1 × 150 K @ 4:50 2 × 75 P @ 1:50 100 EZ **Total: 2,300**		Easy aerobic pace for 30 min	
Wednesday		Easy aerobic pace with cadence at 90 RPM for 60 min		30 min strength training
Thursday	300 S 4 × 50 DR @ 1:15 (odd—R/L single-arm drill[2]; even—3/4 catch-up[1]) 1 × 300 FR @ 6:30 1 × 200 FR @ 4:20 1 × 100 FR @ 2:10 1 × 500 FR @ 10:50 1 × 400 FR @ 8:40 2 × 50 K @ 1:25 100 EZ **Total: 2,200**		Mixed effort (fartlek, or speed play, in which you change up your speed every couple of minutes) on soft trails for 35 min	
Friday	Off	Off	Off	Off
Saturday	Open water with partners for 30 min, focusing on steady aerobic effort, using good form with long strokes, sighting on landmarks, and swimming straight. (If open water is not available, do this workout in a pool, sighting on a landmark above the deck every fourth to sixth stroke.)	Steady state at just below or near goal-race effort for 50 min	Brick run right off the bike for 10 min with focus on breathing and form	
Sunday		Easy aerobic cool-down for 30 min	10 min warm-up, 10 min at goal-race effort, and 10 min easy aerobic cool-down for 30 min	

Bronze-Level Sprint-Distance Triathlon Training Plan
WEEK 8

	Swim	Bike	Run	Strength training
Monday	200 FR 200 DR 50 BLD 3 × 50 K @ 1:15 3 × 200 FR @ 4:15, 4:10, 4:05 4 × 100 FR @ 2:35 2 × 200 FR @ 4:10, 4:05 2 × 50 K @ 1:10 100 EZ **Total: 2,200**			
Tuesday		10 min strong race-pace effort, 10 min smooth easy aerobic effort, and 10 min strong race-pace effort for 30 min	First run (before bike): 5 min easy aerobic warm-up and 5 min strong race-pace effort for 10 min Second run (after bike): 5 min easy aerobic warm-up and 5 min strong race-pace effort for 10 min	
Wednesday		Easy aerobic pace with cadence at 90 for 45 min		
Thursday	300 CH 4 × 50 DR @ 1:15 1 × 500 FR @ 10:15 1 × 400 FR @ 8:15 1 × 300 FR @ 6:10 1 × 200 FR @ 4:10 3 × 50 K @ 1:25 50 EZ **Total: 2,100**		Mixed effort (fartlek, or speed play, in which you change up your speed every couple of minutes) on soft trails for 25 min	
Friday	Off	Off	Off	Off
Saturday	10 min swim. Check out the race swim venue if possible. Do several short accelerations to race-start pace. Be sure to see what the finish area looks like from the water, preferably in the morning near race time.	30 min ride. Ride part of the course. Do a few surges to race pace but keep it mostly under HR zone 3*. Save it for the race.	15 min run. Check out the race start and finish. Stay mainly in HR zone 1–3*, with 3 × 30 sec surges to race pace. Save it for the race.	
Sunday	Race day!			

*To learn more about HR zones, see "Calculating Your Heart Rate" in chapter 7.

Silver-Level Sprint-Distance Triathlon Training Plan
WEEK 1

	Swim	Bike	Run	Strength training
Monday		10 min warm-up at easy aerobic pace; 3 × 10 sec seated sprint, 20 sec recovery spin at easy aerobic pace; then repeat the following for 45 min: seated sprint for 20 sec, recovery spin at easy aerobic pace for 40 sec, seated sprint for 30 sec, and recovery spin at easy aerobic pace for 60 sec		20 min strength training
Tuesday	300 CH 2 times 2 × 100 FR @ 2:00 2 × 150 IM-NF @ 3:20 1 × 200 FR @ 3:40 5 × 50 CH @ :55 (odd—F; even—EZ) 3 × 50 K @ 1:20 50 EZ **Total: 2,600**		Aerobic pace for 35 min	
Wednesday		51 min trainer session: 20 min skill warm-up (3 × 1 min standing big gear, 1 min seated fast spin at >100 cadence, and 6 × 1 min single-leg circular pedaling); 3 × 3 min strong aerobic pace with 1 min easy aerobic pace between; and 10 min light-resistance, high-cadence cool-down		30 min strength training
Thursday	200 FR 200 CH 2 times 2 × 50 K @ 1:15 2 × 100 CH @ 2:05 3 × 150 FR @ 2:45 descending 2 × 100 CH @ 2:05 2 × 50 RB-DPS @ 1:15 50 EZ **Total: 2,550**		5 × 2 min aerobic pace at 80% effort with 2 min easy aerobic pace between for 40 min	
Friday		Aerobic pace on outdoor hills as efficiently as possible and mostly seated and controlled (simulated if inside) for 75 min		
Saturday	200 CH 3 × 150 K-DR-S @ 3:15 3 × 150 DR-S @ 3:00 3 × 150 CH @ 2:50 3 × 150 FR @ 2:40 1 × 500 FR @ 8:45 (1:45) 50 EZ **Total: 2,550**		45 min aerobic	
Sunday			Jog at easy aerobic pace for 20–30 min	

Silver-Level Sprint-Distance Triathlon Training Plan
WEEK 2

	Swim	Bike	Run	Strength training
Monday	Off	Off	Off	Off
Tuesday		Easy aerobic pace for 30 min	Aerobic pace with 6 × 1 min high-cadence, strong aerobic pace and 1 min easy aerobic pace between for 35 min	
Wednesday	100 FR 100 NF 100 CH 4 × 50 CH @ 1:05 descending 3 times 1 × 200 F @ 3:10 2 × 50 EZ-CH @ 1:20 3 × 100 CH @ 2:30 3 times 1 × 200 F @ 3:10 2 × 50 EZ-CH @ 1:20 **Total: 2,600**	Aerobic pace with 4 × 20 sec sprint and 40 sec rest; 3 × 5 min build to strong aerobic pace by 2 min and hold with 3 min easy aerobic pace between for 60 min		
Thursday			8 × 30 sec hill repeats with good form at aerobic pace for 45 min, not a superhard effort, just jogging pace	
Friday	300 CH 4 × 50 CH @ 1:05 4 × 100 CH @ 2:00 1 × 1,500 FR @ 26:15 (1:45) 4 × 100 K @ 2:15 50 EZ **Total: 2,850**			30 min strength training
Saturday		3 × (1 min single leg, 1 min fast spin, 1 min standing) aerobic pace and 2 min easy aerobic pace between for 30 min	Aerobic pace on a hilly course for 60 min	

Sunday	300 CH
	3 × 300 FR @ 6:00
	  descending
	4 × 200 FR @ 3:50
	  descending
	4 × 100 FR @ 2:00
	  descending
	6 × 25 @ :45 (odd—K; even—DR)
	50 EZ
	Total: 2,600
		Easy aerobic pace at high RPM for 70 min		

Silver-Level Sprint-Distance Triathlon Training Plan
WEEK 3

	Swim	Bike	Run	Strength training
Monday		Aerobic pace on trainer with 3 × 3 min strong aerobic for the last 30 min and 5 min threshold pace between for 60 min		20 min strength training
Tuesday	300 FR 200 NF 100 CH 2 times 2 × 50 K @ 1:20 2 × 100 CH-NF @ 2:15 3 × 100 F @ 2:20 2 × 100 CH @ 2:15 2 × 50 DR-S @ 1:10 50 EZ **Total: 2,500**		Easy aerobic pace for 35 min if you feel rested enough, otherwise skip	
Wednesday		Easy aerobic pace with cadence at 90 RPM for 60 min		30 min strength training
Thursday	200 FR 200 CH 4 × 100 K-S @ 2:05 2 times 1 × 300 FR @ 5:15 1 × 200 FR @ 3:20 1 × 100 FR @ 1:35 50 EZ 4 × 100 K @ 2:15 50 EZ **Total: 2,550**		6 × 90 sec aerobic pace on treadmill at 3–4% incline with 2 min easy aerobic pace between for 40 min	
Friday		10, 20, 30 min strong aerobic pace with 10 min aerobic pace between for 90 min		
Saturday	300 CH 3 × 100 K-S @ 2:20 7 × 100 CH @ 2:10 7 × 100 CH @ 2:00 7 × 100 FR @ 1:50 50 EZ **Total: 2,750**		4 × 5 min aerobic pace at 75–80% effort with 5 min easy aerobic pace between for 60 min	
Sunday		Easy aerobic cool-down for 30 min		30 min strength training (optional)

Silver-Level Sprint-Distance Triathlon Training Plan
WEEK 4

	Swim	Bike	Run	Strength training
Monday	Off	Off	Off	Off
Tuesday	200 FR 200 CH 3 × 100 K @ 2:20 3 × 200 CH @ 3:30 3 × 100 K @ 2:10 3 × 150 CH @ 2:30 3 × 100 K @ 2:00 3 × 100 CH @ 1:45 50 EZ **Total: 2,700**	3 × 10, 20, 30 sec seated sprint at easy aerobic pace and 20, 40, and 60 sec recovery spin at easy aerobic pace between for 60 min	Aerobic pace for 40 min	
Wednesday	Off	Off	Off	Off
Thursday	200 FR 100 CH 3 times 100 K @ 2:20 50 DR-S @ 1:05 100 CH @ 1:55 3 times 3 × 50 NF @ 1:05 2 × 50 DPS @ :55 1 × 250 FR @ 3:50 50 EZ **Total: 2,700**	61 min trainer session: 20 min skill warm-up; 5 × 1 min standing big gear and 1 min seated fast spin at >100 cadence; 6 × 1 min single-leg circular pedaling; 10 min at strong aerobic pace; and 15 min light-resistance, high-cadence cool-down	Aerobic pace with the last 5 min at 85% effort for 45 min	
Friday	Off	Off	Off	Off
Saturday	300 CH 8 × 50 @ 1:00 (odd—NF, even—FR) 4 × 100 FR @ 1:40 4 × 100 FR @ 1:50 4 × 100 FR @ 1:40 4 × 100 FR @ 1:50 2 times 1 × 75 K-DR-S @ 1:30 1 × 125 CH @ 2:15 50 EZ **Total: 2,750**	5 × 3 min aerobic pace (big gear, seated and controlled) for 90 min	Aerobic pace for 60 min	
Sunday			Easy aerobic jog for 30 min	20 min strength training

Silver-Level Sprint-Distance Triathlon Training Plan
WEEK 5

	Swim	Bike	Run	Strength training
Monday	Off	Off	Off	Off
Tuesday		Easy aerobic pace for 30 min	Easy aerobic pace for 30 min	
Wednesday	400 CH 6 × 100 K-S @ 2:00 3 × 600 FR @ 10:00, 9:30, 9:00 6 × 25 CH @ :30 50 EZ **Total: 3,000**		Aerobic pace with 8 × 20 sec strides at 90% effort and 40 sec easy aerobic pace between for 45 min	
Thursday		Aerobic pace with 4 × 20 sec sprint and 40 sec rest; 3 × 8 min builds (aerobic pace to strong aerobic pace for the last 3 min) with 2 min easy aerobic pace between for 60 min total		30 min strength training (optional)
Friday	300 CH 2 times 3 × 50 K @ 1:20 (1:25) 2 × 100 FR @ 1:45 (1:55) 1 × 400 FR @ 6:20 (7:00) 2 × 100 NF @ 2.00 (2.10) 3 × 50 DC-DR @ 1:20 (1:25) **Total: 2,500**		Aerobic pace for 30 min	
Saturday		3 × (1 min single leg, 1 min fast spin, 1 min standing) aerobic pace and 2 min easy aerobic pace between for 30 min	Aerobic pace on a hilly course (uphill at 85–90% effort and easy aerobic recovery on the downhill) for 75 min	
Sunday	200 FR 200 CH 2 times 1 × 250 FR @ 3:50 (4:15) 2 × 150 FR @ 2:30 (2:45) 3 × 100 CH @ 1:50 (2:00) 4 × 50 DR @ 1:00 (1:05) 4 × 25 SC @ :35 (:40) **Total: 2,700**	Easy aerobic pace outside for 60 min		

Silver-Level Sprint-Distance Triathlon Training Plan
WEEK 6

	Swim	Bike	Run	Strength training
Monday		Aerobic pace on trainer with 3 × 4 min strong aerobic pace for the last 30 min and 5 min threshold pace between for 60 min		30 min strength training
Tuesday	200 FR 200 CH 3 × 100 K @ 2:20/2:30 3 × 200 CH @ 3:30/3:45 3 × 100 K @ 2:10/2:20 3 × 150 CH @ 2:30/2:40 3 × 100 K @ 2:00/2:10 3 × 100 CH @ 1:45/1:55 50 EZ **Total: 2,700**		Aerobic pace with 7 × 10 sec strides and 20 sec easy aerobic pace between for 30 min	
Wednesday		Easy aerobic pace with heart rate around 120 and cadence at 90 RPM for 45 min		20 min strength training (optional)
Thursday	300 CH 3 × 50 K @ 1:10 3 × 50 DR-S @ 1:00 3 times 3 × 100 DPS @ 1:45 1 × 200 FR @ 3:00 3 × 50 CH @ 1:05 3 × 50 NF @ 1:00 3 × 50 RB-FR @ 1:00 50 EZ **Total: 2,950**		40 min aerobic pace with 15 min at 3–4% incline for 40 min	
Friday		10, 20, 30 min strong aerobic pace with 10 min aerobic pace between for 120 min		
Saturday	300 CH 4 × 100 K @ 2:20 (2:30) 4 × 200 CH @ 3:35 (3:50) 9 × 100 FR @ 1:40 (1:50) 9 × 50 FR @ :50 (:55) 50 EZ **Total: 2,900**		Aerobic pace for 50 min	
Sunday		Easy aerobic cool-down for 30 min		

Silver-Level Sprint-Distance Triathlon Training Plan

WEEK 7

	Swim	Bike	Run	Strength training
Monday		3 × 10, 20, 30 sec seated sprints at easy aerobic pace with 20, 40, and 60 sec recovery spin at easy aerobic pace between for 60 min		20 min strength training
Tuesday	300 S 4 × 50 DR-S @ 1:00 2)(50 F @ :55 1 × 800 @ 12:55 2 × 400 @ 6:30 descending each 100 yards (m) 2 × 300 @ 5:30 (first—P; second—F) 2 × 100 @ 1:50 (first—IM; second—F) 100 EZ **Total: 3,100**		Easy aerobic pace for 30 min	
Wednesday		Easy aerobic pace with cadence at 90 RPM for 75 min		20 min strength training
Thursday	300 S 200 DR 2 × 50 (25 flutter kick, 25 nonflutter kick) 2 × 75 with 10 sec between 50 FR 25 DR 1 × 100 @ 1:25 BLD each 25 1 × 200 EZ @ 3:45 2 × 100 FR @ 1:30 1 × 200 EZ @ 3:45 3 × 100 FR @ 1:35 1 × 200 EZ @ 3:45 4 × 100 FR @ 1:40 1 × 200 EZ @ 3:45 5 × 100 FR @ 1:45 1 × 100 EZ @ 3:45 2 × 25 NF @ :30 F 100 EZ **Total: 3,300**		Mixed effort (fartlek, or speed play, in which you change up your speed every couple of minutes) on soft trails for 40 min	
Friday	Off	Off	Off	Off
Saturday	Open water with partners for 30 min, focusing on steady aerobic effort, using good form with long stroke, sighting on landmarks, and swimming straight. (If open water is not available this week, do the same workout in a pool, sighting on a landmark above the deck every fourth to sixth stroke.)	Steady state at just below or near goal-race effort for 60 min	Brick run right off the bike for 10 min, focusing on breathing and form	
Sunday		Easy aerobic cool-down for 30 min	10 min warm-up, 15 min at goal-race effort and 10 min easy aerobic cool-down for 35 min	

Silver-Level Sprint-Distance Triathlon Training Plan
WEEK 8

	Swim	Bike	Run	Strength training
Monday	300 FR 3 × 100 @ 2:00 (75 FR, 25 K) 1 × 50 DR @ 1:00 (catch-up[1]) 1 × 100 DR @ 1:45 (50 catch-up drill[1], 50 fist drill) 1 × 150 DR @ 2:25 (50 catch-up drill[1], 50 fist drill, 50 fingertip drill) 1 × 200 @ 3:15 (50 catch-up drill[1], 50 fist drill, 50 fingertip drill, 50 triple switch drill[3]) 2 × 300 FR @ 5:50 2 × 300 FR @ 5:45 2 × 300 FR @ 5:40 100 EZ **Total: 3,000**			
Tuesday		10 min strong race-pace effort, 10 min smooth easy aerobic pace, and 10 min strong race-pace effort for 30 min	First run (before bike): 10 min easy aerobic warm-up and 5 min strong race-pace effort for 15 min Second run (after bike): 10 min easy aerobic warm-up and 5 min strong race-pace effort for 15 min	
Wednesday		Easy aerobic pace with cadence at 90 RPM for 60 min		
Thursday	300 S 12 × 50 DR-S @ 1:00 (odd—FR; even—NF) 1 × 600 FR @ 9:00 2 × 300 P @ 4:50 1 × 600 FR @ 8:55 2 × 100 P @ 1:50 2 × 100 K @ 3:25 100 EZ **Total: 3,200**		Mixed effort (fartlek, or speed play, in which you change up your speed every couple of minutes) on soft trails for 30 min	
Friday	Off	Off	Off	Off
Saturday	10 min swim. Check out the race swim venue if possible. Do several short accelerations to race-start pace. Be sure to see what the finish area looks like from the water, preferably in the morning near race time.	30 min ride. Ride part of the course. Do a few surges to race pace, but keep it mostly under HR zone 3*. Save it for the race.	15 min run. Check out the race start and finish. Stay mainly in HR 1–3*, with 3 × 30 sec surges to race pace. Save it for the race.	
Sunday	Race day			

*To learn more about HR zones, see "Calculating Your Heart Rate" in chapter 7.

Gold-Level Sprint-Distance Triathlon Training Plan

WEEK 1

	Swim	Bike	Run	Strength training
Monday			Aerobic pace for 35 min	30 min strength training
Tuesday	400 CH 5 × 250 FR @ 3:45 3 × 100 CH @ 1:50 3 × 250 FR @ 3:30 4 × 100 NF @ 1:45 100 EZ Total: 3,200	3 × 10, 20, 30 sec seated sprints at easy aerobic pace with 20, 40, and 60 sec rest between for 60 min		
Wednesday			Aerobic pace with 5 × 2 min at 80% effort and 2 min easy aerobic between for 40 min total	
Thursday	300 CH 8 × 50 K @ 1:00 7 × 100 CH @ 1:35 6 × 50 K @ :55 5 × 100 CH @ 1:30 4 × 50 K @ :50 3 × 100 CH @ 1:25 2 × 50 K @ :45 1 × 100 CH @ 1:20 100 EZ Total: 3,000	74 min trainer session: 20 min skill warm-up; 5 × 1 min standing big gear and 1 min seated fast spin at >100 cadence; 6 × 1 min single-leg circular pedaling; 3 × 5 min strong aerobic pace with 1 min easy aerobic pace between and 20 min light-resistance, high-cadence cool-down		
Friday			Aerobic pace for 45 min	20 min strength training
Saturday	400 CH 9 × 50 CH @ :55 5 × 100 FR @ 1:30 3 × 250 FR @ 3:35 (1:25) 1 × 500 FR @ 6:40 (1:20) 9 × 50 K @ 1:00 50 EZ Total: 3,100	Aerobic pace on outdoor hills as efficiently as possible and mostly seated and controlled (simulated if inside) for 80 min		
Sunday			Easy aerobic pace for 20–30 min	

Gold-Level Sprint-Distance Triathlon Training Plan
WEEK 2

	Swim	Bike	Run	Strength training
Monday	Off	Off	Off	Off
Tuesday		Easy aerobic pace for 40 min	8 × 1 min high-cadence strong aerobic pace and 1 min easy aerobic pace between for 45 min	
Wednesday	200 FR 200 CH 20 × 50 CH @ :50 20 × 100 CH @ 1:20 50 EZ **Total: 3,450**	Aerobic pace with 4 × 20 sec sprint and 40 sec rest; 4 × 5 min build to strong aerobic pace by 2 min and hold with 3 min easy aerobic pace between for 60 min		
Thursday			10 × 30 sec hill repeats with good form at aerobic pace for 50 min, not a superhard effort, just jogging pace	
Friday	200 FR 200 CH 3 × 100 CH @ 1:40 3 × 300 FR @ 4:30 3 × 100 NF @ 1:50 3 × 300 FR @ 4:15 3 × 100 K @ 2:00 50 EZ **Total: 3,150**			30 min strength training
Saturday		3 × (1 min single leg, 1 min fast spin, 1 min standing) aerobic pace and 2 min easy aerobic pace between for 30 min	Aerobic pace on a hilly course for 60 min	
Sunday	500 CH 3 × 100 IM-NF @ 1:45 7 × 100 FR @ 1:40 (odd—F, even—EZ) 2 × 150 K-DR-S @ 2:40 5 × 100 FR @ 1:30 (odd— F, even—EZ) 1 × 200 CH @ 3:30 3 × 100 FR @ 1:20 (odd—F, even—EZ) 100 EZ **Total: 2,900**	Easy aerobic pace at higher RPM for 90 min		

Gold-Level Sprint-Distance Triathlon Training Plan

Gold WEEK 3

	Swim	Bike	Run	Strength training
Monday	Off	Off	Off	Off
Tuesday	200 FR 200 CH 5 × 50 K @ 1:00 5 × 50 DR-S @ 1:00 4 times 2 × 100 CH @ 1:40 2 × 125 FR @ 1:40 4 × 50 NF @ :55 4 × 50 CH @ :55 50 EZ **Total: 3,150**	Aerobic pace on trainer with 3 × 3 min strong aerobic pace for the last 30 min and 5 min easy aerobic between for 60 min		
Wednesday		Easy aerobic pace for 30 min	Easy aerobic pace for 40 min	
Thursday	400 CH 10 × 100 @ 1:40 (odd—IM-NF, even—CH) 10 × 75 K @ 1:30 12 × 50 @ :55 descending 12 × 25 F @ :30 50 EZ **Total: 3,100**	Easy aerobic pace with cadence at 90 RPM for 90 min		
Friday			8 × 90 sec aerobic pace on treadmill at 4–5% incline with 2 min easy aerobic between for 40 min total, keeping pace around 6.5 mph (10.5 kph)	30 min strength training
Saturday	300 FR 200 CH 4 × 100 K @ 2:05 3 × 100 DR-S @ 1:50 2 × 100 NF @ 1:35 1 × 100 FR @ 1:20 3 × 550 FR @ 8:00, 7:45, 7:30 50 EZ **Total: 3,200**	10, 20, 30 min strong aerobic pace with 10 min aerobic between for 120 min		
Sunday		Easy aerobic cool-down for 30 min	5 × 5 min aerobic pace at 75–80% effort and 5 min easy aerobic between for 70 min	

Gold-Level Sprint-Distance Triathlon Training Plan
WEEK 4

	Swim	Bike	Run	Strength training
Monday		3 × 10, 20, 30 sec seated sprints at easy aerobic pace with 20, 40, and 60 sec rest between for 60 min		20 min strength training
Tuesday	300 CH 1 × 500 FR @ 7:30 (1:30) 10 × 50 CH @ :55 1 × 400 FR @ 5:50 (1:27) 8 × 50 CH @ :50 1 × 300 FR @ 4:15 (1:25) 6 × 50 CH @ :45 1 × 200 FR @ 2:45 (1:22) 4 × 50 CH @ :40 50 EZ **Total: 3,150**		Aerobic pace for 45 min	
Wednesday		71 min trainer session: 20 min skill warm-up; 5 × 1 min standing big gear and 1 min seated fast spin at >100 cadence; 6 × 1 min single-leg circular pedaling; 15 min strong aerobic pace; and 20 min light resistance, high-cadence cool-down		30 min strength training
Thursday	500 CH 4 × 100 CH @ 1:45 1 × 450 P-DPS @ 6:45 1 × 450 DPS @ 6:30 1 × 450 FR @ 6:15 9 × 50 FR @ :45 descending 9 × 50 K @ 1:00 50 EZ **Total: 3,200**		5 min warm-up, 50 min aerobic, and 5 × 2 min building pace to 90% max effort for 65 min	
Friday	Off	Off	Off	Off
Saturday	300 CH 3 × 100 K-SC @ 2:05 2 × 100 DR-S @ 1:50 1 × 100 BLD @ 1:35 8 × 50 CH @ :50 F 1 × 500 RB-DPS @ 8:00 (1:36) 6 × 50 CH @ :45 F 1 × 300 RB-DPS @ 4:45 (1:35) 4 × 50 CH @ :40 F 1 × 100 RB-DPS @ 1:30 2 × 50 CH @ 1:00 F 100 EZ **Total: 2,900**	7 × 3 min aerobic pace (big gear, seated and controlled) for 90 min	Aerobic pace for 90 min	
Sunday			Easy aerobic pace for 30 min	

▼ Gold-Level Sprint-Distance Triathlon Training Plan

Gold WEEK 5

	Swim	Bike	Run	Strength training
Monday			Easy aerobic pace for 40 min	
Tuesday		Easy aerobic pace for 30 min	10 × 20 sec aerobic pace strides at 90% effort and 40 sec easy aerobic between for 45 min	
Wednesday	500 CH 3 times 1 × 150 K-SC-DR @ 3:00 1 × 100 NF @ 1:50 1 × 50 FR @ :45 5 × 100 CH @ 1:40 50 EZ **Total: 3,050**	4 × 20 sec aerobic pace sprint with 40 sec rest between, 3 × 8 min builds (aerobic to strong aerobic pace for the last 3 min) with 2 min easy aerobic between for 60 min		
Thursday			Aerobic pace for 45 min	
Friday	300 CH 3 times 3 × 50 K @ 1:00 3 × 150 SC-DR-S @ 2:45 1 × 100 CH @ 1:20 1 × 100 CH @ 1:30 1 × 100 CH @ 1:40 50 EZ **Total: 3,150**			30 min strength training
Saturday		3 × (1 min single leg, 1 min fast spin, 1 min standing) aerobic pace and 2 min easy aerobic pace between for 30 min total	Aerobic pace on a hilly course for 75 min, going up each hill at 85–90% effort and recovering at easy aerobic pace on the way down	
Sunday	300 CH 5 × 100 CH @ 1:45–1:25 8 × 50 K @ 1:05 4 × 150 CH @ 2:10–1:55 6 × 50 NF @ 1:00 3 × 200 FR @ 2:40–2:30 4 × 50 RB-DPS @ :55 50 EZ **Total: 3,000**	Easy aerobic pace outside for 60 min		

Gold-Level Sprint-Distance Triathlon Training Plan
WEEK 6

	Swim	Bike	Run	Strength training
Monday		Aerobic pace on trainer with 3 × 4 min strong aerobic pace for the last 30 min and 5 min easy aerobic pace between for 60 min		
Tuesday	300 CH 8 × 100 CH @ 1:45 (odd—K-S; even—DR-S) 1 × 1,500 FR @ 21:45 (1:27) descending each 500 8 × 50 CH @ :55 50 EZ **Total: 3,050**		Aerobic pace for 45 min	
Wednesday		Easy aerobic pace for 30 min		30 min strength training
Thursday	300 CH 6 × 100 CH @ 1:35 10 × 75 CH @ 1:20 (even—F) 4 × 100 CH @ 1:35 10 × 50 CH @ :55 (even—F) 2 × 100 CH @ 1:35 10 × 25 CH @ :30 (even—F) 50 EZ **Total: 3,050**	Easy aerobic pace with HR around 120 and cadence at 90 RPM for 90 min total	6 × 2 min aerobic pace at 80% effort with 2 min easy aerobic pace between for 60 min	
Friday	Off	Off	Off	Off
Saturday	300 CH 6 × 100 CH @ 1:35 10 × 75 CH @ 1:20 (even—F) 4 × 100 CH @ 1:35 10 × 50 CH @ :55 (even—F) 2 × 100 CH @ 1:35 10 × 25 CH @ :30 (even—F) 50 EZ **Total: 3,050**	10, 20, 30 min strong aerobic pace with 10 min aerobic pace between for 120 min	Aerobic pace for 60 min	
Sunday		Easy aerobic cooldown for 30 min	Easy aerobic pace for 20–30 min	

Gold-Level Sprint-Distance Triathlon Training Plan
WEEK 7

	Swim	Bike	Run	Strength training
Monday		3 × 10, 20, 30 sec easy aerobic seated sprints with 20, 40, and 60 sec rest between for 60 min		30 min strength training (optional)
Tuesday	4 × 100 (50 smooth, 25 BLD, 25 F) 6 × 50 DR @ 1:05 3 × 50 FR @ :55 2 × 25 FR @ :30 1 × 50 CH @ 1:00 50 EZ 4 × 50 FR @ :50 3 × 25 FR @ :30 1 × 75 CH @ 1:15 50 EZ 5 × 50 FR @ :45 4 × 25 FR @ :25 1 × 100 FR @ 1:30 100 EZ 1 time 400 P @ 5:30 300 K-S by 50 meter S @ 5:00 4 × 25 BLD @ :30 2 × 25 sprint @ :30 1 × 200 @ 3:00 (rest 10 sec each 50) 200 EZ @ no time limit, focus on execution (25 K, 25 DR, 50 EZ) **Total: 3,200**		Easy aerobic pace for 30 min	
Wednesday		Easy aerobic pace with cadence at 90 RPM for 90 min		
Thursday	300 S 200 NF 2 × 50 BLD 4 × 125 @ 1:55 (50 DR, 75 S) 1 × 400 @ 6:00 (100 DR, 100 K, 100 DR, 100 smooth) 1 × 400 @ 6:00 (100 buildup, 100 build down, 200 hard) 1 × 400 @ 6:00 (build up every 100, full sprint last 25) 4 times 1 × 100 FR @ 1:30 descending 1 × 150 CH @ 2:00 (recovery) 100 EZ **Total: 3,400**		Mixed effort (fartlek, or speed play, in which you change up your speed every couple of minutes) on soft trails for 45 min	
Friday	Off	Off	Off	Off
Saturday	Open water with partners for 20 min, focusing on steady aerobic effort using good form with long stroke, sighting on landmarks, and swimming straight. (If open water is not available this week, do the same workout in a pool, sighting on a landmark above the deck every fourth to sixth stroke.)	60 min steady state at just below or near goal-race effort	15 min brick run right off the bike, focusing on breathing and form	
Sunday		Easy aerobic cool-down for 30 min	10 min warm-up at aerobic pace, 20 min at goal-race effort, and 10 min easy aerobic cool-down for 40 min total	

Gold-Level Sprint-Distance Triathlon Training Plan
WEEK 8

	Swim	Bike	Run	Strength training

Monday	300 S
	150 K
	1 × 50 BLD
	6 × 75 @ 1:15 (descending stroke count for 1–3, descending time for 4–6)
	10 × 150—
	  1–3 FR @ 2:15
	  4–6 FR @ 2:25, 2:15, 2:05 (descending)
	  7–8 FR @ 2:20 (100 at 70% max effort; 50 at race pace)
	  9–10 @ 2:15 (50 at 70% max effort, 100 at race pace)
	2 × 150 CH @ 2:30 (1st = 25 DR, 25 FR, 25 DR, 25 FR, 25 DR, 25 FR; 2nd = 75 K, 75 DR)
	150 EZ
	Total: 2,900			

Tuesday		10 min strong race-pace effort, 10 min smooth easy aerobic effort, and 10 min strong race-pace effort for 30 min	First run (before bike): 10 min easy aerobic warm-up and 5 min strong race-pace effort for 15 min total Second run (after bike): 10 min easy aerobic warm-up and 5 min strong race-pace effort for 15 min total	
Wednesday		Easy aerobic pace with cadence at 90 RPM for 60 min		

	Swim	Bike	Run	Strength training
Thursday	200 FR 200 IM-NF 100 K 100 P 8 × 50 @ 1:00 (odd—25 DR, 25 EZ; even—25 BLD, 25 EZ) 1 × 100 @ 1:55 sprint (goal to touch the wall @ 1:25) 1 × 100 EZ @ 1:40 1 × 100 @ 1:55 sprint (goal to touch the wall @ 1:25) 1 × 200 EZ @ 3:20 1 × 100 @ 1:55 sprint (goal to touch the wall @ 1:25) 1 × 300 FR @ 5:00 1 × 100 @ 1:55 sprint (goal to touch the wall @ 1:25) 1 × 400 FR @ 6:40 1 × 100 @ 1:55 sprint (goal to touch the wall @ 1:25) 1 × 500 smooth @ 7:30 (RB every 4–5 strokes) 100 EZ **Total: 3,100**		Mixed effort (fartlek, or speed play, in which you change up your speed every couple of minutes) on soft trails for 30 min	
Friday	Off	Off	Off	Off
Saturday	10 min swim. Check out the race swim venue if possible. Do several short accelerations to race-start pace. Be sure to see what the finish area looks like from the water, preferably in the morning near race time.	30 min ride. Ride part of the course. Do a few surges to race pace, but keep it mostly under HR zone 3*. Save it for the race.	15 min run. Check out the race start and finish. Stay mainly in HR 1–3*, with 3 × 30 sec surges to race pace. Save it for the race.	
Sunday	Race day			

*To learn more about HR zones, see "Calculating Your Heart Rate" in chapter 7.

CHAPTER 11

STANDARD-DISTANCE TRIATHLON TRAINING PLANS

Now that you have completed your first sprint race and have built up your endurance and fitness, you might want to consider a standard-distance triathlon for a bigger challenge. In this chapter, we discuss the basics of the standard-distance triathlon and provide training plans for bronze-, silver-, and gold-level athletes.

Standard-Distance Triathlon Basics

Training for a standard-distance triathlon is similar to training for a sprint race. Many of the workout types and tapering methods translate from one distance to the other. The main difference is that you will be training for an event that is twice as long, so we need to increase the volume of training in each discipline. An easy solution would be simply to double the workouts, but we can do better than that. A specific balance of volume and intensity will give you the best opportunity to achieve your goals.

- *Swim*: Again, you will likely swim in a 25-meter or 25-yard pool. Follow the plan and swim yards or meters; it doesn't matter which. As with the sprint triathlon, each standard-distance plan consists of a warm-up, main set, and cool-down. Ideally, you will find a place to swim in the open water a few times before race day so that you become familiar with swimming in a straight line without having a line at the bottom of the pool to follow. The swim workouts are given in distance as well as goal pace. If you can't reach that pace, don't worry; you can adjust those paces as needed.

- *Bike*: Some of the bike workouts are prescribed for outdoors; others are prescribed for the trainer. The bike workouts are prescribed in time with a warm-up, main set, and cool-down. Specific drills, hills, and sprints are also prescribed. If you need to move a prescribed outdoor ride indoors, you should convert the overall time by a factor of .75. For example, a prescribed 60-minute road ride would translate to a 45-minute trainer ride.

- *Run*: The running workouts again are prescribed in time and effort at certain paces. Some of the workouts are prescribed for the treadmill, using the incline for hills, and others are prescribed for outside. Your situation and schedule will determine when you choose to run outdoors versus indoors. Don't lock yourself into a specific mode of running. You should switch things up no matter where you live.

Training for a standard-distance triathlon should start 8 weeks before the race date, although you can start 12 weeks before the race if time permits. As with the sprint-training model, you will gradually increase how often you train (frequency), how long each training session is (duration), and how hard each workout is (intensity) as you move into the weeks closer to race day.

- A bronze-level athlete should train between 7 and 9 hours per week.

- A silver-level athlete should train between 8 and 10 hours per week.

- A gold-level athlete should train between 9 and 11 hours per week.

For the days when two workouts are prescribed, you should keep at least 3 to 4 hours between the swim, bike, and run workouts, unless a brick workout (back-to-back sessions) is prescribed. You can do a strength session following any of the swim, bike, and run workouts prescribed for that day to save time. Or you can split up the day and do your swim, bike, or run in the morning and strength training in the evening. With the greater volume and intensity, spacing out your workouts becomes more important. Likewise, you must be sure to fuel and hydrate sufficiently to maintain proper nutrient levels and balances. Refer to chapter 9 for details on nutrition.

If you are brand new to our sport in all aspects, this is the best place for you to start. If after a few days or weeks, this program feels too easy for you, take things up a notch to the silver level. The programs parallel each other, so you can simply shift and stay at the same point in the training program.

You may want to customize these plans further. For example, if you are a bronze-level swimmer but a silver-level runner, you can replace the run segment of the bronze plan with the silver plan. You can replace part of one plan with another if you are stronger or weaker in a sport.

In addition, although the plans in this chapter specify the days of the week to perform each workout and space them out to allow adequate rest and recovery, the plan is flexible and can be modified to meet your scheduling needs. For example, if you need to move the swim workouts from Tuesday, Thursday, and Saturday to Wednesday, Friday, and

Sunday, you can do so. You would then just switch the bike and run workout days as well. In short, don't be afraid to pull from different workout levels based on your strengths and weaknesses. If you are still frustrated with this type of personalization, we recommend you contact a professional coach to help you modify the programs we have provided.

Sample Standard-Distance Triathlon Plans

We offer sample 8-week standard-distance triathlon plans for bronze-level, silver-level, and gold-level athletes. The programs are designed based on experience and exposure to many athletes of various abilities. The specific periodization and tapering methods used in these programs allow you sufficient rest and recovery to take you to your race day in the best possible fitness.

Note that the following workouts are written using a type of shorthand. The more you swim, the more accustomed you will become to interpreting it. For example, 3×100 FR @ 2:40 is read "3 by 100 free on the 2:40." This means that you do three repetitions of 100 yards (m) in which each 100-yard swim, along with a small bit of rest, should occur within 2 minutes and 40 seconds. Should you not be able to swim the 100 yards and have at least 10 seconds of rest inside the 2:40, feel free to stretch out these times a bit further. Each interval is designed to have a bit of rest. Also, when the table reads "3 times" that means to repeat what is below it that number of times. A key of the shorthand can be found on the part III opener. There are three drills that appear in these tables that are not described in the chapters of this book. The descriptions for those drills are below.

[1]Catch-up drill: This drill focuses on timing. As one hand enters the water and extends forward, it remains in this position until the opposite hand enters and touches the original hand. At that moment the original hand begins a catch, pull, recovery, and entry then touching the opposite hand signaling its turn to catch, pull, exit, recovery, and enter again. Using a swim aid such as a kick board can help with the hand switching. The kick board will remain in front of you while you essentially pass it back and forth between lead hands. The use of fins or a pull buoy during this drill can help with extra buoyancy.

[2]Single-arm drill: This drill allows you to focus on one side of the body at a time. Begin with extending your nonbreathing-side hand straight forward, then execute a normal swim stroke and breathing pattern with the single arm. For example if you are breathing on your right side, your left hand is stretched out and does not move as your right hand executes a normal swim stroke cycle. Switch hands and breathing sides every length. The use of fins or a pull buoy during this drill can help with extra buoyancy.

[3]Triple switch drill: This drill is similar to the single-arm drill, where you will make three swim stroke cycles with your right hand, take three normal two-handed swim stroke cycles, then three swim stroke cycles with only your left hand while your right hand is stretched out forward, back to three, two-handed normal swim stroke cycles, then three single-arm stroke cycles with your right hand only. Repeat this pattern for the entire swim length.

Bronze-Level Standard-Distance Triathlon Training Plan
WEEK 1

	Swim	Bike	Run	Strength training
Monday	Off	Off	Off	Off
Tuesday	200 CH 1 × 400 FR @ 10:00 (2:30) 6 × 50 CH @ 1:20 1 × 300 FR @ 7:00 (2:20) 4 × 50 CH @ 1:15 1 × 200 FR @ 4:30 (2:15) 2 × 50 CH @ 1:10 1 × 100 FR @ 2:10 50 EZ **Total: 1,850**		Aerobic pace for 30 min	
Wednesday		3 × 10, 20, 30 sec seated sprints at easy aerobic pace with 20, 40, and 60 sec rest between for 45 min		
Thursday	200 CH 2 × 150 K-DR-S @ 4:30 2 × 150 DR-S @ 4:20 2 × 150 CH @ 4:10 2 × 150 FR @ 4:00 1 × 500 FR @ 12:15 (2:15) 50 EZ **Total: 1,950**			30 min strength training
Friday		40 min trainer session: 10 min skill warm-up (3 × 1 min standing big gear, 1 min seated fast spin at >100 cadence, and 1 min single-leg circular pedaling); 3 × 3 min at strong aerobic pace with 2 min easy aerobic pace between; and 12 min light-resistance, high-cadence cool-down	4 × 2 min at 80% aerobic pace effort with 2 min easy aerobic pace between for 35 min —or— 5 min aerobic pace run and 1 min walk, following the pattern for 35 min	
Saturday	100 FR 100 CH 3 × 50 CH @ 1:30 descending 3 times 1 × 200 F @ 4:00 2 × 50 EZ-CH @ 2:00 3 × 50 CH @ 2:00 3 times 1 × 200 F @ 4:00 2 × 50 EZ-CH @ 2:00 **Total: 2,300**			30 min strength training (optional)
Sunday		Aerobic pace on hills as efficiently as you can, mostly seated and controlled (simulated if inside) for 60 min	Aerobic run for 6 min with 2 min walk between for 35 min	

Bronze-Level Standard-Distance Triathlon Training Plan
WEEK 2

	Swim	Bike	Run	Strength training
Monday	Off	Off	Off	Off
Tuesday		Easy aerobic pace for 30 min	4 × 1 min high cadence strong aerobic pace with 1 min easy aerobic pace between for 35 min	
Wednesday	200 CH 2 times 1 × 100 FR @ 2:30 1 × 150 IM-NF @ 4:15 1 × 200 FR @ 4:30 5 × 50 CH @ 1:10 (odd—F; even—EZ) 3 × 50 K @ 1:45 50 EZ **Total: 2,000**			30 min strength training
Thursday		4 × 20 sec aerobic pace sprint with 40 sec rest, 2 × 5 min build to strong aerobic by 2 min and hold with 3 min easy aerobic between for 60 min	6 × 30 sec aerobic pace hill repeats with good form for 30 min	
Friday	200 FR 100 CH 2 times 1 × 50 K @ 1:40 1 × 100 CH @ 2:40 3 × 150 FR @ 3:40 descending 1 × 100 CH @ 2:40 1 × 50 RB-DPS @ 1:40 50 EZ **Total: 1,850**			30 min strength training (optional)
Saturday			Aerobic pace for 40 min	
Sunday	100 FR 100 CH 3 × 50 CH @ 1:30 descending 3 times 1 × 200 F @ 4:00 2 × 50 EZ-CH @ 2:00 3 × 50 CH @ 2:00 3 times 1 × 200 F @ 4:00 2 × 50 EZ-CH @ 2:00 **Total: 2,300**	3 × (1 min single leg, 1 min fast spin, 1 min standing) at aerobic pace with 2 min easy aerobic pace between for 80 min		

Bronze-Level Standard-Distance Triathlon Training Plan
WEEK 3

	Swim	Bike	Run	Strength training
Monday	Off	Off	Off	Off
Tuesday	200 FR 100 CH 3 × 100 K-S @ 2:30 2 times 1 × 200 FR @ 4:45 1 × 150 FR @ 3:30 1 × 100 FR @ 2:15 50 EZ 3 × 100 K @ 2:45 50 EZ **Total: 1,950**		Easy aerobic pace for 30 min if you feel rested enough; otherwise skip	
Wednesday		Aerobic pace on trainer with 3 × 3 min strong aerobic pace for the last 30 min and 5 min threshold pace between for 45 min		30 min strength training
Thursday	200 FR 150 NF 100 CH 2 times 2 × 50 K @ 1:30 1 × 100 CH-NF @ 2:20 2 × 100 F @ 2:30 1 × 100 CH @ 2:20 2 × 50 DR-S @ 1:30 50 EZ **Total: 1,750**		4 × 90 sec aerobic pace on treadmill at 2–3% incline with 3 min easy aerobic between for 30 min	
Friday		Easy aerobic pace with cadence at 90 for 60 min		30 min strength training
Saturday	200 CH 2 × 50 K-DR @ 2:00 2 times 3 × 100 FR @ 2:40 2 × 50 CH @ 1:30 2 × 100 FR @ 2:20 1 × 50 CH @ 1:40 1 × 100 FR @ 2:00 50 EZ **Total: 1,900**	10 min warm-up at easy aerobic pace, 20 min strong aerobic pace, 10 min aerobic pace, 20 min strong aerobic pace, 10 min aerobic pace, and 20 min strong aerobic pace for 90 min	3 × 5 min aerobic pace at 75–80% effort with 5 min easy aerobic pace between for 45 min	
Sunday		Easy aerobic cool-down for 30 min		

Bronze-Level Standard-Distance Triathlon Training Plan
WEEK 4

	Swim	Bike	Run	Strength training
Monday	Off	Off	Off	Off
Tuesday	100 FR 100 CH 3 × 100 CH @ 2:25 3 × 100 FR @ 2:20, 2:15, 2:10 3 × 100 CH @ 2:30 2 × 150 FR 3:30, 3:15 3 × 100 CH @ 2:35 1 × 200 FR @ 4:00 50 EZ **Total: 1,950**	3 × 10, 20, 30 sec seated sprints at easy aerobic pace with 20, 40, and 60 sec rest between for 40 min	Aerobic pace for 35 min	
Wednesday	Off	Off	Off	Off
Thursday	200 CH 1 × 300 FR @ 6:45 (2:15) 2 × 200 FR @ 4:25 (2:12) 3 × 150 FR @ 3:15 (2:10) 3 × 100 FR @ 2:05 4 × 50 K @ 1:45 50 EZ **Total: 1,900**	60 min trainer session: 10 min easy aerobic spin, 10 min skill warm-up (5 × 1 min standing big gear and 1 min seated fast spin at >100 cadence); 2 × 5 min at strong aerobic pace with 5 min aerobic pace between; and 20 min light-resistance, high-cadence cool-down	Aerobic pace for 50 min with the last 5 mins at 85% effort	
Friday				30 min strength training
Saturday	100 FR 100 CH 3 times 50 K @ 1:30 50 DR @ 1:25 50 CH @ 1:20 3 × 200 FR @ 4:30 descending 3 times 50 SC @ 1:30 50 NF @ 1:20 50 FR @ 1:10 3 × 100 FR @ 2:15 descending 50 EZ **Total: 2,050**		Run at aerobic pace for 8 min with 2 min walk between for 60 min	
Sunday		5 × 3 min bigger gear seated and controlled aerobic pace (don't crush it; just use slower cadence) for 70 min	40 min jog at easy aerobic pace	

Bronze-Level Standard-Distance Triathlon Training Plan
WEEK 5

	Swim	Bike	Run	Strength training
Monday	Off	Off	Off	Off
Tuesday		Easy aerobic pace for 30 min	Easy aerobic pace for 30 min	
Wednesday	200 FR 150 NF 100 CH 5 × 50 DR @ 1:30 4 × 50 SC-K @ 1:40 3 × 50 DPS-RB @ 1:20 2 × 200 FR @ 5:30 descending 50 EZ **Total: 1,700**		6 × 20 sec aerobic pace strides at 90% effort with 40 sec easy aerobic pace between for 45 min	
Thursday		4 × 20 sec aerobic pace sprint with 40 sec rest between, 3 × 5 min builds (aerobic to strong aerobic for the last 3 min) with 2 min easy aerobic pace between for 45 min		30 min strength training
Friday	200 CH 4 × 75 CH @ 1:45 2 times 1 × 50 K @ 1:30 2 × 50 CH @ 1:20 3 × 50 CH @ 1:10 1 × 250 FR @ 4:45 50 EZ 4 × 75 DPS-RB @ 1:45 50 EZ **Total: 2,050**		Easy aerobic pace for 20 min	
Saturday		3 × (1 min single leg, 1 min fast spin, 1 min standing) at aerobic pace with 2 min easy aerobic pace between for 40 min	Aerobic pace on a hilly course (uphill at 85–90% effort and easy aerobic recovery on the downhill) for 70 min	
Sunday	200 CH 3 × 100 K-SC-DR-S @ 1:50 3 times 2 × 50 BLD @ 1:10 1 × 100 CH @ 2:20 2 × 50 F @ 1:05 1 × 150 DPS @ 3:30 4 × 50 K @ 1:30 50 EZ **Total: 2,000**	Easy aerobic pace outside for 60 min		

Bronze-Level Standard-Distance Triathlon Training Plan
WEEK 6

	Swim	Bike	Run	Strength training
Monday		Aerobic pace on trainer with 3 × 4 min strong aerobic pace for the last 30 min and 5 min threshold pace between for 60 min		
Tuesday	200 FR 100 CH 3 × 100 K @ 2:30–2:40 2 × 200 CH @ 1:05 1:30 2 × 100 K @ 2:20–2:30 2 × 150 CH @ 2:55–3:20 1 × 100 K @ 2:20–2:30 2 × 100 CH @ 2:05–2:15 50 EZ **Total: 1,850**		5 × 10 sec aerobic pace strides with 20 sec easy aerobic pace between for 30 min	
Wednesday		Easy aerobic pace with cadence at 90 RPM for 30 min		30 min strength training
Thursday	200 FR 100 CH 2 times 1 × 150 FR @ 3:05 (3:20) 2 × 125 FR @ 2:45 (3:00) 2 × 100 CH @ 2:25 (2:40) 3 × 50 DR @ 1:20 (1:25) 4 × 25 SC @ :45 (:45) **Total: 2,000**		Walk or jog at aerobic pace with 10 min at 3–4% incline for 40 min	
Friday		10 min easy aerobic pace warm-up, 20 min strong aerobic pace, 10 min aerobic pace, 20 min strong aerobic pace, 10 min aerobic pace, 20 min strong aerobic pace for 90 min		
Saturday	200 CH 2 times 2 × 50 K @ 1:30 (1:35) 2 × 100 FR @ 2:15 (2:25) 1 × 250 FR @ 5:20 (5:45) 2 × 100 NF @ 2:30 (2:40) 2 × 50 SC-DR @ 1:30 (1:35) **Total: 1,900**		Aerobic pace for 50 min	
Sunday		Aerobic pace on trainer with 3 × 4 min strong aerobic pace for the last 30 min and 5 min threshold pace between for 75 min		30 min strength training

Bronze-Level Standard-Distance Triathlon Training Plan
WEEK 7

	Swim	Bike	Run	Strength training
Monday		3 × 10, 20, 30 sec seated sprints at easy aerobic pace with 20, 40, and 60 sec rest between for 60 min		30 min strength training
Tuesday	200 FR 100 K 100 NF 8 × 25 DR @ :40 (do NF and FR drills) 3 × 100 FR @ 2:15 4 times 1 × 125 CH @ 2:50 1 × 75 @ 2:00 (25 K, 50 CH) 1 × 50 @ 1:25 (alternate FR and NF per 50) 1 × 150 K @ 4:50 2 × 75 P @ 1:50 100 EZ **Total: 2,300**		Easy aerobic pace for 30 min	
Wednesday		Easy aerobic pace with cadence at 90 for 60 min		30 min strength training
Thursday	300 S 4 × 50 DR @ 1:15 (odd—R/L single arm[2]; even—3/4 catch-up[1]) 1 × 300 FR @ 6:30 1 × 200 FR @ 4:20 1 × 100 FR @ 2:10 1 × 500 FR @ 10:50 1 × 400 FR @ 8:40 2 × 50 K @ 1:25 100 EZ **Total: 2,200**		Mixed effort (fartlek, or speed play, in which you change up your speed every couple of minutes) on soft trails for 35 min	
Friday	Off	Off	Off	Off
Saturday	Open water with partners for 30 min, focusing on steady aerobic effort, using good form with long strokes, sighting on landmarks, and swimming straight. (If open water is not available, do this workout in a pool, sighting on a landmark above the deck every fourth to sixth stroke.)	Steady state at just below or near goal-race effort for 60 min	Brick run right off the bike for 10 min with focus on breathing and form	
Sunday		Easy aerobic cool-down ride for 30 min	10 min warm-up, 10 min at goal-race effort, and 10 min easy aerobic cool-down for 30 min	

Bronze-Level Standard-Distance Triathlon Training Plan

WEEK 8

	Swim	Bike	Run	Strength training
Monday	200 FR 200 DR 50 BLD 3 × 50 K @ 1:15 3 × 200 FR @ 4:15, 4:10, 4:05 4 × 100 (odd—IM @ 2:35; even—FR @ 2:00) 2 × 200 FR @ 4:10, 4:05 2 × 50 K @ 1:10 100 EZ **Total: 2,200**			
Tuesday		10 min strong race-pace effort, 10 min smooth easy aerobic effort, and 10 min strong race-pace effort for 30 min	First run (before bike): 5 min easy aerobic warm-up and 5 min strong race-pace effort for 10 min Second run (after bike): 5 min easy aerobic warm-up and 5 min strong race-pace effort for 10 min	
Wednesday		Easy aerobic pace with cadence at 90 RPM for 45 min		
Thursday	300 CH 4 × 50 DR @ 1:15 1 × 500 FR @ 10:15 1 × 400 FR @ 8:15 1 × 300 FR @ 6:10 1 × 200 FR @ 4:10 3 × 50 K @ 1:25 50 EZ **Total: 2,100**		Mixed effort (fartlek, or speed play, in which you change up your speed every couple of minutes) on soft trails for 20 min	
Friday	Off	Off	Off	Off
Saturday	10 min swim. Check out the race swim venue if possible. Do several short accelerations to race-start pace. Be sure to see what the finish area looks like from the water, preferably in the morning near race time.	30 min ride. Ride part of the course. Do a few surges to race pace, but keep it mostly under your threshold.	15 min run. Check out the race start and finish. Stay mainly in HR 1–3*, with 3 × 30 sec surges to race pace.	
Sunday	Race day			

*To learn more about HR zones, see "Calculating Your Heart Rate" in chapter 7.

Silver-Level Standard-Distance Triathlon Training Plan

Silver   WEEK 1

	Swim	Bike	Run	Strength training
Monday		3 × 10, 20, 30 sec seated sprints at aerobic pace with 20, 40, and 60 sec easy aerobic between for 45 min		30 min strength training
Tuesday	300 CH 2 times 2 × 100 FR @ 2:00 2 × 150 IM-NF @ 3:20 1 × 200 FR @ 3:40 5 × 50 CH @ :55 (odd—F; even—EZ) 3 × 50 K @ 1:20 50 EZ **Total: 2,600**		4 × 20 sec builds (aerobic pace to strong aerobic) with 40 sec easy aerobic between for 35 min	
Wednesday		45 min trainer session: 20 min skill warm-up (3 × 1 min standing big gear, 1 min seated fast spin at >100 cadence, and 5 × 1 min single-leg circular pedaling); 3 × 3 min at strong aerobic pace with 1 min easy aerobic pace between; and 13 min light-resistance, high-cadence cool-down		30 min strength training
Thursday	200 FR 200 CH 2 times 2 × 50 K @ 1:15 2 × 100 CH @ 2:05 3 × 150 FR @ 2:45 descending 2 × 100 CH @ 2:05 2 × 50 RB-DPS @ 1:15 50 EZ **Total: 2,550**		5 × 2 min aerobic pace at 80% effort and 2 min easy aerobic pace between for 40 min	
Friday		Aerobic pace on outdoor hills as efficiently as possible and mostly seated and controlled (simulated if inside) for 90 min		
Saturday	200 CH 3 × 150 K-DR-S @ 3:15 3 × 150 DR-S @ 3:00 3 × 150 CH @ 2:50 3 × 150 FR @ 2:40 1 × 500 FR @ 8:45 (1:45) 50 EZ **Total: 2,550**		Aerobic pace for 45 min	
Sunday			Jog at easy aerobic pace for 30–40 min	

Silver-Level Standard-Distance Triathlon Training Plan
WEEK 2

	Swim	Bike	Run	Strength training
Monday	Off	Off	Off	Off
Tuesday		Easy aerobic pace for 40 min	Aerobic pace with 6 × 1 min strong aerobic pace at a high cadence and 1 min easy aerobic pace between for 35 min	
Wednesday	100 FR 100 NF 100 CH 4 × 50 CH @ 1:05 descending 3 times 1 × 200 F @ 3:10 2 × 50 EZ-CH @ 1:20 3 × 100 CH @ 2:30 3 times 1 × 200 F @ 3:10 2 × 50 EZ-CH @ 1:20 **Total: 2,600**	4 × 20 sec sprint at aerobic pace with 40 sec rest between and 3 × 5 min build to strong aerobic pace by 2 min and hold with 3 min easy aerobic pace between for 75 min		
Thursday			8 × 30 sec hill repeats with good form at aerobic pace for 45 min, not a superhard effort, just jogging pace	
Friday	300 CH 4 × 50 CH @ 1:05 4 × 100 CH @ 2:00 1 × 1,500 FR @ 26:15 (1:45 per 100) 4 × 100 K @ 2:15 50 EZ **Total: 2,850**			30 min strength training
Saturday		3 × (1 min single leg, 1 min fast spin, 1 min standing) at aerobic pace with 2 min easy aerobic pace between for 30 min	Aerobic pace on a hilly course for 60 min	

Sunday	300 CH
	3 × 300 FR @ 6:00
	  descending
	4 × 200 FR @ 3:50
	  descending
	4 × 100 FR @ 2:00
	  descending
	6 × 25 @ :45 (odd—K; even—DR)
	50 EZ
	Total: 2,600
		Easy aerobic pace at higher RPM for 80 min		

Silver-Level Standard-Distance Triathlon Training Plan
WEEK 3

	Swim	Bike	Run	Strength training
Monday		60 min trainer session: 3 × 3 min aerobic pace with strong aerobic pace for the last 30 min and 5 min threshold pace between for 60 min		30 min strength training
Tuesday	300 FR 200 NF 100 CH 2 times 2 × 50 K @ 1:20 2 × 100 CH-NF @ 2:15 3 × 100 F @ 2:20 2 × 100 CH @ 2:15 2 × 50 DR-S @ 1:10 50 EZ **Total: 2,500**		Easy aerobic pace for 35 min if you feel rested enough; otherwise skip	
Wednesday		Easy aerobic pace with cadence at 90 RPM for 75 min		30 min strength training
Thursday	200 FR 200 CH 4 × 100 K-S @ 2:05 2 times 1 × 300 FR @ 5:15 1 × 200 FR @ 3:20 1 × 100 FR @ 1:35 50 EZ 4 × 100 K @ 2:15 50 EZ **Total: 2,550**		6 × 90 sec aerobic pace on treadmill at 3–4% incline with 2 min easy aerobic pace between for 45 min	
Friday		10 min warm-up at easy aerobic pace, then 10 min strong aerobic pace, 10 min easy aerobic pace, 20 min strong aerobic pace, 10 min easy aerobic, pace, 30 min strong aerobic pace with 10 min easy aerobic pace between for 100 min		
Saturday	300 CH 3 × 100 K-S @ 2:20 7 × 100 CH @ 2:10 7 × 100 CH @ 2:00 7 × 100 FR @ 1:50 50 EZ **Total: 2,750**		4 × 5 min aerobic pace at 75–80% effort with 5 min easy aerobic pace between for 65 min	
Sunday		Easy aerobic cool-down for 40 min		

Silver-Level Standard-Distance Triathlon Training Plan
WEEK 4

	Swim	Bike	Run	Strength training
Monday	Off	Off	Off	Off
Tuesday	200 FR 200 CH 3 × 100 K @ 2:20 3 × 200 CH @ 3:30 3 × 100 K @ 2:10 3 × 150 CH @ 2:30 3 × 100 K @ 2:00 3 × 100 CH @ 1:45 50 EZ **Total: 2,700**	3 × 10, 20, 30 sec seated sprints at easy aerobic pace with 20, 40, and 60 sec easy aerobic pace between for 60 min	4 × 20 sec builds (aerobic pace to strong aerobic pace) with 40 sec easy aerobic pace between for 40 min	
Wednesday				30 min strength training
Thursday	200 FR 100 CH 3 times 100 K @ 2:20 50 DR-S @ 1:05 100 CH @ 1:55 3 times 3 × 50 NF @ 1:05 2 × 50 DPS @ :55 1 × 250 FR @ 3:50 50 EZ **Total: 2,700**	45 min trainer session: 10 min easy aerobic spin, 10 min skill warm-up (5 × 1 min standing big gear and 1 min seated fast spin at >100 cadence); 5 × 1 min single-leg circular pedaling; 10 min strong aerobic pace; and 15 min light-resistance, high-cadence cool-down	Aerobic pace for 45 min with the last 5 min at 85% effort	
Friday				30 min strength training

Saturday	300 CH
	8 × 50 @ 1:00 (odd—NF, even—FR)
	16 × 100—
	  4 × 100 FR @ 1:40
	  4 × 100 FR @ 1:50
	  4 × 100 FR @ 1:40
	  4 × 100 FR @ 1:50
	2 times
	1 × 75 K-DR-S @ 1:30
	1 × 125 CH @ 2:15
	50 EZ
	Total: 2,750
		5 × 4 min aerobic pace (big gear, seated and controlled) for 90 min	Aerobic pace for 70 min	

Sunday			Jog at easy aerobic pace for 30 min	

Silver-Level Standard-Distance Triathlon Training Plan
WEEK 5

	Swim	Bike	Run	Strength training
Monday	Off	Off	Off	Off
Tuesday		Easy aerobic pace for 40 min	Easy aerobic pace with low heart rate for 30 min	
Wednesday	400 CH 6 × 100 K-S @ 2:00 3 × 600 FR @ 10:00, 9:30, 9:00 6 × 25 CH @ :30 50 EZ **Total: 3,000**		8 × 20 sec aerobic pace strides at 90% efforts with 40 sec easy aerobic pace between for 45 min	
Thursday		4 × 20 sec sprint at aerobic pace with 40 sec easy aerobic pace between, 3 × 8 min builds (aerobic pace to strong aerobic for the last 3 min) with 2 min easy aerobic pace between for 80 min		30 min strength training
Friday	300 CH 2 times 3 × 50 K @ 1:20 (1:25) 2 × 100 FR @ 1:45 (1:55) 1 × 400 FR @ 6:20 (7:00) 2 × 100 NF @ 2:00 (2:10) 3 × 50 SC-DR @ 1:20 (1:25) **Total: 2,500**		Aerobic pace for 30 min	
Saturday		3 × (1 min single leg, 1 min fast spin, and 1 min standing) aerobic pace with 2 min easy aerobic pace between for 40 min	Aerobic pace on a hilly course (uphill at 85–90% effort and easy aerobic recovery on the downhill) for 75 min	
Sunday	200 FR 200 CH 2 times 1 × 250 FR @ 3:50 (4:15) 2 × 150 FR @ 2:30 (2:45) 3 × 100 CH @ 1:50 (2:00) 4 × 50 DR @ 1:00 (1:05) 4 × 25 SC @ :35 (:40) **Total: 2,700**	Easy aerobic pace outside for 60 min		

Silver-Level Standard-Distance Triathlon Training Plan
WEEK 6

	Swim	Bike	Run	Strength training
Monday		Aerobic pace on trainer with 3 × 4 min strong aerobic pace for the last 30 min and 5 min threshold pace between for 60 min		
Tuesday	200 FR 200 CH 3 × 100 K @ 2:20 3 × 200 CH @ 3:30 3 × 100 K @ 2:10 3 × 150 CH @ 2:30 3 × 100 K @ 2:00 3 × 100 CH @ 1:45 50 EZ **Total: 2,700**		7 × 10 sec strides at aerobic pace with 20 sec easy aerobic pace between for 30 min	
Wednesday		Easy aerobic pace with heart rate around 120 and cadence at 90 RPM for 45 min		30 min strength training
Thursday	300 CH 3 × 50 K @ 1:10 3 × 50 DR-S @ 1:00 3 times 3 × 100 DPS @ 1:45 1 × 200 FR @ 3:00 3 × 50 CH @ 1:05 3 × 50 NF @ 1:00 3 × 50 RB-FR @ 1:00 50 EZ **Total: 2,950**		Jog at easy aerobic pace with 15 min at 3–4% incline for 40 min	
Friday		10, 20, 30 min strong aerobic pace with 10 min aerobic pace between for 120 min		
Saturday	300 CH 4 × 100 K @ 2:20 (2:30) 4 × 200 CH @ 3:35 (3:50) 9 × 100 FR @ 1:40 (1:50) 9 × 50 FR @ :50 (:55) 50 EZ **Total: 2,900**		Aerobic pace for 60 min	
Sunday		Easy aerobic cool-down for 40 min		

Silver-Level Standard-Distance Triathlon Training Plan

WEEK 7

	Swim	Bike	Run	Strength training
Monday		3 × 10, 20, 30 sec seated sprints at easy aerobic pace with 20, 40, and 60 sec easy aerobic pace between for 60 min		30 min strength training
Tuesday	300 S 4 × 50 DR-S @ 1:00 2 × 50 F @ :55 1 × 800 F @ 12:55 2 × 400 @ 6:30 descending 2 × 300 @ 5:30 (first—P; second—F) 2 × 100 @ 1:50 (first—IM; second—F) 100 EZ **Total: 3,100**		4 × 20 sec builds (easy aerobic pace to strong aerobic pace) with 40 sec easy aerobic pace between for 30 min	
Wednesday		Easy aerobic pace with cadence at 90 RPM for 75 min		
Thursday	300 S 200 DR 2 × 50 with 10 sec between (25 flutter kick, 25 nonflutter kick) 2 × 75 with 10 sec between (25 S, 25 DR, 25 FR BLD) 1 × 100 FR @ 1:25 1 × 200 EZ @ 3:45 2 × 100 FR @ 1:30 1 × 200 EZ @ 3:45 3 × 100 FR @ 1:35 1 × 200 EZ @ 3:45 4 × 100 FR @ 1:40 1 × 200 EZ @ 3:45 5 × 100 FR @ 1:45 1 × 100 EZ @ 3:45 2 × 25 NF-F @ :30 100 EZ **Total: 3,300**		Mixed effort (fartlek, or speed play, in which you change up your speed every couple of minutes) on soft trails for 40 min	

	Swim	Bike	Run	Strength training
Friday	Off	Off	Off	Off
Saturday	Open water with partners for 30 min, focusing on steady, aerobic effort, using good form with long strokes, sighting on landmarks, and swimming straight. (If open water is not available, do the workout in a pool, sighting on a landmark above the deck every fourth to sixth stroke.)	Steady state at just below or near goal-race effort for 70 min	Brick run right off the bike for 10 min with focus on breathing and form	
Sunday		Easy aerobic cool-down for 40 min	10 min warm-up, 15 min at goal-race effort, and 10 min easy aerobic cool-down for 35 min	

Silver-Level Standard-Distance Triathlon Training Plan
WEEK 8

	Swim	Bike	Run	Strength training
Monday	300 S 3 × 100 @ 2:00 (75 S, 25 K) 1 × 50 DR catch-up[1] @ 1:00 1 × 100 DR @ 1:45 (50 catch-up[1], 50 fist) 1 × 150 DR @ 2:25 (50 catch-up[1], 50 fist, 50 fingertip) 1 × 200 DR @ 3:15 (50 catch-up[1], 50 fist, 50 fingertip, 50 triple switch[3]) 2 × 300 FR @ 5:50 2 × 300 FR @ 5:45 2 × 300 FR @ 5:40 100 EZ **Total: 3,000**			
Tuesday		10 min strong race-pace effort, 10 min smooth easy aerobic effort, and 10 min strong race-pace effort for 30 min	First run (before bike): 10 min easy aerobic warm-up and 5 min strong race-pace effort for 15 min Second run (after bike): 10 min easy aerobic warm-up and 5 min strong race-pace effort for 15 min	
Wednesday		Easy aerobic pace with cadence at 90 RPM for 60 min		
Thursday	300 S 12 × 50 DR-S @ 1:00 (odd—FR, even—NF) 1 × 600 FR @ 9:00 2 × 300 P @ 4:50 1 × 600 FR @ 8:55 2 × 100 P @ 1:50 2 × 100 K @ 3:25 100 EZ **Total: 3,200**		Mixed effort (fartlek, or speed play, in which you change up your speed every couple of minutes) on soft trails for 30 min	
Friday	Off	Off	Off	Off
Saturday	10 min swim. Check out the race swim venue if possible. Do several short accelerations to race-start pace. Be sure to see what the finish area looks like from the water, preferably in the morning near race time.	30 min ride. Ride part of the course. Do a few surges to race pace but keep it mostly under HR zone 3*.	15 min run. Check out the race start and finish. Stay mainly in HR zone 1–3*, with 3 × 30 sec surges to race.	
Sunday	Race day			

*To learn more about HR zones, see "Calculating Your Heart Rate" in chapter 7.

Gold-Level Standard-Distance Triathlon Training Plan

WEEK 1

	Swim	Bike	Run	Strength training
Monday			4 × 20 sec builds (aerobic to strong aerobic pace) with 40 sec easy aerobic pace between for 35 min	
Tuesday	400 CH 5 × 250 FR @ 3:45 3 × 100 CH @ 1:50 3 × 250 FR @ 3.30 4 × 100 NF @ 1:45 100 EZ **Total: 3,200**	3 × 10, 20, 30 sec seated sprints at easy aerobic pace with 20, 40, and 60 sec easy aerobic pace between for 60 min		
Wednesday			5 × 2 min aerobic pace at 80% effort with 2 min easy aerobic pace between for 40 min	
Thursday	300 CH 8 × 50 K @ 1:00 7 × 100 CH @ 1:35 6 × 50 K @ :55 5 × 100 CH @ 1:30 4 × 50 K @ :50 3 × 100 CH @ 1:25 2 × 50 K @ :45 1 × 100 CH @ 1:20 100 EZ **Total: 3,000**	60 min trainer session: 10 min warm-up at easy aerobic pace, 10 min skill warm-up (5 × 1 min standing big gear and 1 min seated fast spin at >100 cadence); 5 × 1 min single-leg circular pedaling; 3 × 5 min at strong aerobic pace with 1 min easy aerobic pace between; and 17 min light-resistance, high-cadence cool-down		
Friday			Aerobic pace for 45 min	
Saturday	400 CH 9 × 50 CH @ :55 5 × 100 FR @ 1:30 3 × 250 FR @ 3:35 (1:25) 1 × 500 FR @ 6:40 (1:20) 9 × 50 K @ 1:00 50 EZ **Total: 3,100**	Aerobic pace on outdoor hills as efficiently as possible and mostly seated and controlled (simulated if inside) for 90 min		
Sunday			Jog at easy aerobic pace for 20–30 min	

Gold-Level Standard-Distance Triathlon Training Plan
WEEK 2

	Swim	Bike	Run	Strength training
Monday	Off	Off	Off	Off
Tuesday		Easy aerobic pace for 40 min	8 × 1 min high-cadence strong aerobic pace and 1 min easy aerobic pace between for 45 min	
Wednesday	200 FR 200 CH 20 × 50 CH @ :50 20 × 100 CH @ 1:20 50 EZ **Total: 3,450**	4 × 20 sec sprint at aerobic pace with 40 sec easy aerobic pace between, 4 × 5 min builds to strong aerobic pace by 2 min and hold with 3 min easy aerobic between for 75 min		30 min strength training
Thursday			10 × 30 sec hill repeats with good form at aerobic pace for 50 min, not a superhard effort, just jogging pace	
Friday	200 FR 200 CH 3 × 100 CH @ 1:40 3 × 300 FR @ 4:30 3 × 100 NF @ 1:50 3 × 300 FR @ 4:15 3 × 100 K @ 2:00 50 EZ **Total: 3,150**			
Saturday		3 × (1 min single leg, 1 min fast spin, 1 min standing) at aerobic pace with 2 min easy aerobic pace between for 30 min	Aerobic pace on a hilly course for 60 min	
Sunday	500 CH 3 × 100 IM-NF @ 1:45 7 × 100 FR @ 1:40 (odd—F) 2 × 150 K-DR-S @ 2:40 5 × 100 FR @ 1:30 (odd—F) 1 × 200 CH @ 3:30 3 × 100 FR @ 1:20 (odd—F) 100 EZ **Total: 2,900**	Easy aerobic pace at higher RPM for 105 min		

Gold-Level Standard-Distance Triathlon Training Plan

WEEK 3

	Swim	Bike	Run	Strength training
Monday	Off	Off	Off	Off
Tuesday	200 FR 200 CH 5 × 50 K @ 1:00 5 × 50 DR-S @ 1:00 4 times 2 × 100 CH @ 1:40 2 × 125 FR @ 1:40 4 × 50 NF @ :55 4 × 50 CH @ :55 50 EZ **Total: 3,150**	60 min trainer session: 3 × 3 min aerobic pace to strong aerobic pace for the last 30 min and 5 min easy aerobic pace between		30 min strength training
Wednesday		Easy aerobic pace for 30 min	4 × 20 sec builds (aerobic pace to strong aerobic pace) with 40 sec easy aerobic pace between for 40 min	
Thursday	400 CH 10 × 100 @ 1:40 (odd—IM-NF; even—CH) 10 × 75 K @ 1:30 12 × 50 @ :55 descending each 4 12 × 25 F @ :30 50 EZ **Total: 3,100**	Easy aerobic pace with cadence at 90 RPM for 90 min		
Friday			8 × 90 sec aerobic pace (about 6.5 mph [10.5 kph]) on treadmill at 4–5% incline and 2 min easy aerobic pace between for 40 min	
Saturday	300 FR 200 CH 4 × 100 K @ 2:05 3 × 100 DR-S @ 1:50 2 × 100 NF @ 1:35 1 × 100 FR @ 1:20 3 × 550 FR @ 8:00, 7:45, 7:30 50 EZ **Total: 3,200**	10 min easy aerobic pace, 10 min strong aerobic pace, 10 min easy aerobic pace, 20 min strong aerobic pace, 10 min easy aerobic pace, 30 min strong aerobic pace with 10 min aerobic pace between for 100 min		30 min strength training
Sunday		Easy aerobic cool-down for 40 min	5 × 5 min aerobic pace at 75–80% effort with 5 min easy aerobic pace between for 70 min	

Gold-Level Standard-Distance Triathlon Training Plan

WEEK 4

	Swim	Bike	Run	Strength training
Monday		3 × 10, 20, 30 sec seated sprints at easy aerobic pace with 20, 40, and 60 sec easy aerobic recovery between for 60 min		
Tuesday	300 CH 1 × 500 FR @ 7:30 (1:30) 10 × 50 CH @ :55 1 × 400 FR @ 5:50 (1:27) 8 × 50 CH @ :50 1 × 300 FR @ 4:15 (1:25) 6 × 50 CH @ :45 1 × 200 FR @ 2:45 (1:22) 4 × 50 CH @ :40 50 EZ **Total: 3,150**		Aerobic pace for 45 min	
Wednesday		Begin with easy aerobic pace for 5 min, then shift gears as follows: 2 min easy aerobic 30 sec strong aerobic @ 53 × 15* 30 sec easy aerobic 30 sec strong aerobic @ 53 × 12 30 sec easy aerobic 60 sec strong aerobic @ 53 × 15 30 sec easy aerobic 90 sec strong aerobic @ 53 × 18 30 sec easy aerobic 60 sec strong aerobic @ 53 × 15 30 sec easy aerobic 30 sec strong aerobic @ 53 × 12 2 min easy spin Next, race tempo for 5 min and shift into a different gear every 20 sec, as follows: 2 min easy spin 5 times 15 sec @ 53 × 18 15 sec @ 53 × 15 15 sec @ 53 × 12 15 sec easy spin 2 min easy spin 3 × 30 sec strong aerobic @ 53 × 14 (20 sec seated build intensity, 10 sec standing sprint) with 30 sec easy aerobic between 5–10 min cool-down at easy aerobic pace	30 min strength training	

	Swim	Bike	Run	**Strength training**
Thursday	500 CH 4 × 100 CH @ 1:45 3 × 450 @ 6:45 (P-DPS), 6:30 (DPS), 6:15 9 × 50 @ :45 (descending 3, 3, 2, 1) 9 × 50 K @ 1:00 50 EZ **Total: 3,200**			
Friday	Off	Off	Off	Off
Saturday	300 CH 3 × 100 K-SC @ 2:05 2 × 100 DR-S @ 1:50 1 × 100 BLD @ 1:35 8 × 50 CH @ :50 F 1 × 500 RB-DPS @ 8:00 (1:36) 6 × 50 CH @ :45 F 1 × 300 RB-DPS @ 4:45 (1:35) 4 × 50 CH @ :40 F 1 × 100 RB-DPS @ 1:30 2 × 50 CH @ 1:00 F 100 EZ **Total: 2,900**	7 × 4 min (seated and controlled, bigger gear) at aerobic pace for 90 min	Aerobic pace for 90 min	
Sunday			Jog at easy aerobic pace for 30 min	

*The gear ratio your bike should be in during the particular set. The first number, 53, refers to the number of teeth in the largest chain ring on the front of your bike, and the second number refers to a specific gear on the rear cassette cluster. We refer to the smallest cog on your rear cassette as 12 and the largest as 21; 15 is approximately in the middle of the cluster, and 18 is about 2 cogs down from the largest cog on the rear cassette cluster.

Gold-Level Standard-Distance Triathlon Training Plan

Gold WEEK 5

	Swim	Bike	Run	Strength training
Monday			4 × 20 sec builds (aerobic pace to strong aerobic pace) with 40 sec easy aerobic pace between for 40 min	30 min strength training
Tuesday		Easy aerobic pace for 30 min	10 × 20 sec aerobic pace strides at 90% effort and 40 sec easy aerobic between for 45 min	
Wednesday	500 CH 3 times 1 × 150 K-SC-DR @ 3:00 1 × 100 NF @ 1:50 1 × 50 FR @ :45 5 × 100 CH @ 1:40 50 EZ **Total: 3,050**	4 × 20 sec aerobic sprint with 40 sec rest between, 3 × 8 min build (aerobic pace to strong aerobic pace for the last 3 min) with 2 min easy aerobic pace between for 80 min		
Thursday			Aerobic pace for 45 min	
Friday	300 CH 3 times 3 × 50 K @ 1:00) 3 × 150 SC-DR-S @ 2:45 3 × 100 CH @ 1:20, 1:30, 1:40 50 EZ **Total: 3,150**			30 min strength training
Saturday		3 × (1 min single leg, 1 min fast spin, 1 min standing) aerobic pace and 2 min easy aerobic between for 40 min	Aerobic pace on a hilly course (uphill at 85–90% effort and easy aerobic recovery on the downhill) for 80 min	
Sunday	300 CH 5 × 100 CH @ 1:45–1:25 8 × 50 K @ 1:05 4 × 150 CH @ 2:10–1:55 6 × 50 NF @ 1:00 3 × 200 FR @ 2:40–2:30 4 × 50 RB-DPS @ :55 50 EZ **Total: 3,000**	Easy aerobic pace outside for 90 min		

Gold-Level Standard-Distance Triathlon Training Plan

WEEK 6

	Swim	Bike	Run	Strength training
Monday		60 min trainer session: 3 × 4 min aerobic pace to strong aerobic pace for the last 30 min with 5 min easy aerobic pace between		
Tuesday	300 CH 8 × 100 CH @ 1:45 (odd— K S; ouon DR F) 1 × 1,500 FR @ 21:45 (1:27) descending each 500 8 × 50 CH @ :55 50 EZ **Total: 3,050**		4 × 20 sec builds (aerobic pace to strong aerobic pace) with 40 sec easy aerobic pace between for 45 min	
Wednesday		Easy aerobic pace for 40 min		30 min strength training
Thursday	300 CH 6 × 100 CH @ 1:35 10 × 75 CH @ 1:20 (even—F) 4 × 100 CH @ 1:35 10 × 50 CH @ :55 (even—F) 2 × 100 CH @ 1:35 10 × 25 CH @ :30 (even—F) 50 EZ **Total: 3,050**	10 min easy aerobic pace, 10 min strong aerobic pace, 10 min easy aerobic pace, 20 min strong aerobic pace, 10 min easy aerobic pace, 30 min strong aerobic pace, 10 min easy aerobic pace for 100 min.	6 × 2 min aerobic pace at 80% effort with 2 min easy aerobic pace between for 60 min	
Friday	Off	Off	Off	Off
Saturday	300 CH 6 × 100 CH @ 1:35 10 × 75 CH @ 1:20 (even—F) 4 × 100 CH @ 1:35 10 × 50 CH @ :55 (even—F) 2 × 100 CH @ 1:35 10 × 25 CH @ :30 (even—F) 50 EZ **Total: 3,050**	10, 20, 30 min strong aerobic pace with 10 min aerobic pace between for 120 min	Aerobic pace for 75 min	
Sunday		Easy aerobic cool-down for 40 min	Jog at easy aerobic pace for 20–30 min	

Gold-Level Standard-Distance Triathlon Training Plan
WEEK 7

	Swim	Bike	Run	Strength training
Monday		3 × 10, 20, 30 sec seated sprints at easy aerobic pace with 20, 40, and 60 sec easy aerobic pace between for 60 min		30 min strength training

Tuesday	400 S (50 smooth, 25 BLD, 25 F)
	6 × 50 DR @ 1:05
	3 × 50 FR @ :55
	2 × 25 FR @ :30
	1 × 50 CH @ 1:00
	50 EZ
	4 × 50 FR @ :50
	3 × 25 FR @ :30
	1 × 75 CH @ 1:15
	50 EZ
	5 × 50 FR @ :45
	4 × 25 FR @ :25
	1 × 100 FR @ 1:30
	100 EZ
	1 × 700—
	   400 P @ 5:30
	   300 as (50 K, 50 F-FR) @ 5:00
	4 × 25 BLD @ :30
	2 × 25 F @ :30
	1 × 200 @ 3:00 with 10 sec rest after each 50, hold interval at 3:00
	200 EZ (25 K, 25 DR, 50 EZ)
	Total: 3,200
			4 × 20 sec builds (aerobic pace to strong aerobic pace) with 40 sec easy aerobic pace between for 30 min	

Wednesday		Easy aerobic pace with cadence at 90 RPM for 90 min		

	Swim	Bike	Run	Strength training
Thursday	300 S 200 NF 2 × 50 BLD 4 × 125 @ 1:55 (50 DR, 75 S) 1 × 400 @ 6:00 (100 DR, 100 K, 100 DR, 100 smooth) 1 × 400 @ 6:00 (100 BLD up 25, 100 BLD down 25, 200 hard) 1 × 400 @ 6:00 (BLD up every 100; last 25 full sprint) 4 times 1 × 100 FR @ 1:30 descending 1 × 150 CH-EZ @ 2:00 100 EZ **Total: 3,400**			30 min strength training
Friday	Off	Off	Off	Off
Saturday	Open water with partners for 30 min, focusing on steady aerobic effort, using good form with long strokes, sighting on landmarks, and swimming straight. (If open water is not available, do the workout in a pool, sighting on a landmark above the deck every fourth to sixth stroke.)	Steady state at just below or near goal-race effort for 60 min	Brick run right off the bike for 25 min with focus on breathing and form	
Sunday		Easy aerobic cool-down for 40 min	15 min warm-up, 30 min at goal-race effort, and 15 min easy aerobic cool-down for 60 min	

Gold-Level Standard-Distance Triathlon Training Plan
WEEK 8

	Swim	Bike	Run	Strength training

Monday	300 S
	150 K
	1 × 50 BLD
	6 × 75 @ 1:15 (1–3 descending stroke count; 4–6 descending time)
	10 × 150—
	  1–3 @ 2:15
	  4–6 @ 2:25, 2:15, 2:05 descending
	  7–8 @ 2:20 (100 moderate [70% effort], 50 race effort)
	  9–10 @ 2:15 (50 moderate [70% effort], 100 race effort)
	2 × 150 CH @ 2:30 (first—25 DR, 25 S; second—75 K, 75 DR)
	150 EZ
	Total: 2,900			

Tuesday		10 min strong race-pace effort, 10 min smooth easy aerobic effort, and 10 min strong race-pace effort for 30 min	First run (before bike): 10 min easy aerobic warm-up and 5 min strong race-pace effort for 15 min Second run (after bike): 10 min easy aerobic warm-up and 5 min strong race-pace effort for 15 min	
Wednesday		Easy aerobic pace with cadence at 90 RPM for 60 min		

	Swim	Bike	Run	Strength training
Thursday	200 FR 200 IM-NF 100 K 100 P 8 × 50 @ 1:00 (odd—25 DR, 25 EZ-S; even—25 BLD up, 25 EZ) 1 × 100 sprint @ 1:55 (in @ 1:25) 1 × 100 EZ @ 1:40 1 × 100 sprint @ 1:55 (in @ 1:25) 1 × 200 EZ @ 3:20 1 × 100 sprint @ 1:55 (in @ 1:25) 1 × 300 EZ @ 5:00 1 × 100 sprint @ 1:55 (in @ 1:25) 1 × 400 EZ @ 6:40 1 × 100 sprint @ 1:55 (in @ 1:25) 1 × 500 smooth @ 7:30 (RB every four to five strokes) 1 × 100 EZ **Total: 3,100**		Mixed effort (fartlek, or speed play, in which you change up your speed every couple of minutes) on soft trails for 30 min	
Friday	Off	Off	Off	Off
Saturday	10 min swim. Check out the race swim venue if possible. Do several short accelerations to race-start pace. Be sure to see what the finish area looks like from the water, preferably in the morning near race time.	30 min ride. Ride part of the course. Do a few surges to race pace but keep it mostly under HR zone 3*.	15 min run. Check out the race start and finish. Stay mainly in HR zone 1–3*, with 3 × 30 sec surges to race pace.	
Sunday	Race day			

*To learn more about HR zones, see "Calculating Your Heart Rate" in chapter 7.

PART IV

RACING

CHAPTER 12

PREPARING TO RACE

Up to this point we have been focusing on single aspects of your first race. Now you need to begin to put it all together for the big day. Preparing for race day is not a 1-day process. It starts 1 to 2 weeks out, and you need a plan to execute it, just as you need a plan to perform your triathlon training for the swim, bike, and run. The plan can be flexible the further out you start, but as you near the time you hit the water, you have less and less wiggle room. For that reason, you need to give your preparation plan plenty of thought. We will discuss everything from what you wear, to how to get your bike ready, to what to pack for transition and everything in between.

Choosing Your Clothing for the Race

By the time you're 2 to 3 weeks out from race day, you should have picked out your race outfit including shoes, socks, shorts, and shirt. You need to have these items selected this far in advance so that you can practice in them and determine whether they are comfortable and don't cause you any problems. One of our favorite mottos is "Never try something new on race day." Race clothing, like race nutrition, is personal; although something works for or is preferred by one person, it may not be the best thing for everyone. With that in mind, we want to outline why we choose what we wear on race day.

We suggest that you choose a day when you can wear everything you plan to race in and do a complete workout. Your outfit should be comfortable and should not irritate any part of your body. If it does, now is the time to correct it or replace it. Simply washing the clothing can often soften up the seams and eliminate any unwanted rubbing or irritation. If that doesn't work, try some antichafing agent, like Body Glide, on the area. Likely irritation zones are near uniform seams, in your groin or crotch, around your neck, and the inside of your upper arms. If you are planning to use a wetsuit, remember not to use Vaseline or any other petroleum-based lubricant because it will break down the neoprene and you will end up with a bunch of black melted goop on your body.

PROTECTING AGAINST HOT SPOTS

Antichafing agents come in three basic forms—stick, cream, and spray. A stick-style agent looks and feels much like underarm deodorant. It can be applied anywhere on the body. Keep these products out of extreme heat because they will melt. The stick style will be less likely to wash away during the swim portion of your race and will give you longer-lasting protection compared with the other two styles. A cream-style product is normally applied only to the chamois of your shorts in either biking or triathlon. A cream gives the maximum amount of protection in this area, but it often becomes diluted and disappears shortly after the swim. Spray-on lubricants are convenient and can be applied to any part of the body. They are resistant to water but cannot be caked on in areas that require more protection. A spray can work well in conjunction with a stick-style antichafing agent. We suggest you play around with all three types and see which you like best. Many brands are on the market; pick one or a couple and see how each works for you. A new trend is for these products to be hypoallergenic, which obviously helps if you have sensitive skin.

Preparing Your Bike for the Race

The next item you'll need to ensure is in proper working order is your bike. At first glance, a bike may appear to be in good working condition, but some issues may not be obvious and you don't want to take chances come race day. At least 2 weeks before the race, schedule a tune-up with your local bike shop. Do not leave this task until the last minute because during the summer and on heavy race weekends, everyone else has the same idea. A good tune-up includes inspection and adjustment of the brakes and all cables, inspection and lubrication of your chain, adjustment of your shifting, a check of your tires, and tightening of all bolts.

Nothing is more frustrating than training for an event and then having an equipment issue during the race. A skipping chain or broken cable can put a serious damper on what should have been an epic day. Going forward, we suggest that you ask your local bike shop about introductory mechanics classes and learn how to do some simple bike maintenance yourself. Knowing how to identify and execute simple adjustments can save you time and money in the long run.

USA Triathlon/Rich Cruse

Make sure your bike is ready for race day.

At the beginning of each triathlon season (typically spring), it's a good idea to take your bike in for a tune-up as well. The more you ride your bike, the more maintenance and upkeep it will require, much like your car. Listen for any unique sounds that your bike is making and have them looked at early. Ultimately, two tune-ups per year should be adequate, but you could increase this number based on distance ridden.

Picking Up Your Race Packet

About 5 days out from your race you should take a deep dive into the event website and ensure that the timelines you had originally understood to be true have not changed. You would be surprised how often expo times, packet pickup locations, or start times are modified because of unforeseen issues. If your race has early packet pickup opportunities, we suggest you do it. You can check one more thing off your list and reduce some of the anxiety on race morning. When choosing a best time to do your packet pickup, think about what everyone else is doing. Lunch hour is likely one of the busiest times. Just as busy is the rush that comes when most people are leaving work. By avoiding those times you will most likely avoid the lines. You don't need to be first in line; it's not as if you're camping out for concert tickets, and the race won't run out of shirts. Play it smart, and you will be sure to zip in and out.

When picking up your packet, you will want to bring your state-issued identification or driver's license as well as your USA Triathlon membership card. Without these, you will not be able to pick up your race packet. If you are an annual member and do not have your physical USAT member card, you can print a temporary card at www.teamusa.org/usa-triathlon or use the USAT mobile app to show that your membership is current and valid. If your plan was to have someone else pick up your packet for you, or if you were planning to pick up someone else's, you will likely be out of luck. USA Triathlon–sanctioned races mandate that athletes pick up their own packets for insurance purposes. We agree that this policy is an inconvenience, but as they say, "It is what it is." Most packet pickups are located in affiliated triathlon or bike stores or the host hotel for the event. If packet pickup is in a triathlon or bike store, you would have a chance to pick up any last-minute supplies you may need like Body Glide, extra goggles, a hat or visor, or some gels.

Traveling to Your Race

About 3 days out from the race you should begin to think about your travel route and timeline for getting to the race. A quick check of the map should give you a good idea of the best route to take and the travel time required to get to your event. Note that some races close local roads, so the easiest path to the race may not be available. Do not plan on crossing the bike or run course as you get to the race. Local road construction can also cause havoc on race morning, but doing a quick check or asking questions about traffic routes when you pick up your packet should help you avoid this issue. Allow yourself an extra 15 to 30 minutes in the morning to find a parking spot and do anything else that may come up. Parking can be at a premium around race venues. Having a few spots in mind before you leave can help you avoid wasting time driving around. Remember that everyone is trying to get to the same place you are.

Hydrating for Your Race

The day before your race, plan to keep a water bottle with you at all times. Hydration is a key to a positive race result, and being well hydrated starts the day before your race. Take small sips throughout the day and begin to monitor your urine output. You should be urinating about once every hour to hour and a half. Your urine should be a pale yellow and should not have much, if any, odor. Urine that is yellow to dark yellow and is odorous is an early sign of dehydration. Increase your water consumption and keep monitoring for a change. We suggest water during this day over most sports drinks because most sports drinks contain a large amount of sugar.

Prepping Your Equipment for the Race

Around noon the day before your race, lay out all the equipment you plan to take to the race. We advise you to do this in the morning or afternoon because if you are missing anything, you can go shopping during the day. You don't want to find out that your goggles are broken at 10 o'clock on a Saturday night. If that is the case, you are in a bit of trouble. If you eliminate the issues early, you won't panic.

Figure 12.1 is a standard checklist of items you will want to bring to your race. We suggest you copy it so that you can use it multiple times. If you can laminate it and keep it in your triathlon equipment bag, that would be even better. A race-day equipment checklist should be personalized, but we think that the following items are essential to take with you to the start of the race. You can adapt and modify this list to meet your specific needs.

The way you get everything to the race is a more personal choice. Triathlon-specific bags offer dry compartments for your wetsuit and soggy clothes after the race as well as shoe compartments that prevent dirt from getting on your clothes.

PASTA PARTIES

Some events have large pasta feeds or carbo-loading parties. Although these events can be fun to attend, they can also cause you to overeat or eat too late in the day. The original concept of carbo loading was created in the 1970s during the marathon boom. The idea was to eat a large amount of carbohydrate 48 hours before an endurance event and then fast the following day. Over time this concept has been misunderstood and has led to digestive problems in athletes on race day. At your first race we want you to experience everything triathlons have to offer, so we won't tell you to stay home. We will suggest you go early, sit at a table where you can make some new friends, and eat only a normal portion. If dessert is offered, you can have one, but be sure to keep it small. Focus on the community aspect of the event and engage in conversations with other triathletes.

Figure 12.1   Race-Day Equipment Checklist

General

____USAT membership card

____Photo ID

____Registration confirmation

____Directions to venue

____Course map

____Money

____Race uniform

____Race numbers and timing chip

____Sunscreen

____Sunglasses

____Anti-chafing product

____Extra clothes

____Watch

Transition gear

____Towel(s)/Transition mat

____Water bottle(s)

____Gels/Energy bars and drinks/Salt tablets

Swim gear

____Wetsuit

____Swim cap

____Goggles

____Nose plugs

Bike gear

____Bike

____Helmet

____Bike shoes

____Bike gloves

____Tire pump

____Spare tube(s)

____CO_2 cartridges

____Tools

____Bar-end plugs

Run gear

____Running shoes

____Hat/visor

____Race number belt

____Socks

From USAT, 2017, *Train to Tri: Your First Triathlon* (Champaign, IL: Human Kinetics)

Planning and Preparing the Night Before Your Race

The night before your race is important. As we said at the beginning of this chapter, the closer you move toward the race start, the more important things become. Do not overlook your prerace meal or dinner.

Assuming that your race starts at a typical time in the early morning, you will want to eat at around 6:00 or 6:30 the night before. Eating at home is your best option, if it's possible. A simple meal consisting of carbohydrate and protein is your best plan. Do not stuff yourself; you should eat a normal portion just like on any other day. Avoid heavy red meats that may not digest quickly; these foods can cause stomach distress or a heavy feeling during your race. Also, avoid raw meats, sushi, or any other foods that you have never tried before.

We suggest that you avoid drinking alcohol during dinner. Although one glass of wine or a beer won't kill you, why chance it? You'll have plenty of time to celebrate after the race.

After dinner, do one last check of your race list and then pack your bag. A triathlon bag needs to be well thought out. The bag should be a backpack style so that you can ride your bike with your bag on your back to the race start. You'll want to find a bag with a dry compartment to separate your wet clothes from your dry clothes. It should be waterproof in case of rain and not so large that you can't carry it. Make sure to write your name on it in case other athletes have the same bag. In the past you were allowed to store your transition bag next to where you set up your transition. Now, most races have a bag check where you store your bags outside of transition after you drop off your necessary items. This system helps keep transition clear and is safer for everyone, but it can cause a bit of anxiety. If the race requires you to check your transition bag, you should check it on your way down to the swim start. If you are allowed to keep your transition bag in transition, be aware that you might not be able to access it immediately following your race so that the transition area remains clear for athletes still racing. Race directors usually allow athletes back in to get their gear after the last cyclist has come through transition and is out on the run course. If you have specific questions regarding transition access during your race, check with the race director or the race website for details and times that you are allowed in and out of transition.

We have discussed everything you need to do leading up to race day, preparations on the final day, the meal the night before, and your equipment and clothing checklist. Now all that is left for you to do is fall asleep. Because you might be a little nervous the night before the race, you need to sleep well the two nights before your race. If you don't rest well the night before, don't worry about it; adrenaline and the experience of your first triathlon will get you through the race. Before you fall asleep, be sure to set your alarm for the next morning.

In the next chapter we discuss what to expect during your race-day experience, how to execute your race plan, what your backup plan should be in case things don't go as expected, and how to adjust your strategy on the fly.

CHAPTER 13

YOUR RACE-DAY EXPERIENCE

Congratulations—you have made it to your race day! You've done all the preparation of training, your nutrition is dialed in, and you are ready to race! As you wake you are no doubt feeling some butterflies in your tummy. This is a good thing; nervous energy can either cripple you or propel you. We are going to help you make it the latter by walking you through a few possible race-day experiences. We'll talk about how to plan your day, what to expect, and how to establish a backup plan in case things do not go as smoothly as you have planned. Most important, trust that the training you have done and everything you have learned in this book has set you up for the best race you can possibly have. Keep positive thoughts as you move through your day and be confident in the knowledge that you have done the work. The race is simply the victory lap.

Now, let's start walking through what you are most likely to experience on your big day.

Preparing on the Morning of Your Race

On race morning you should begin with a moderate breakfast. Try to eat a normal meal about 3 hours before the start of the event. So, for example, if your race starts at 7:00 a.m., you need to set your alarm to wake up and eat around 4:00 a.m. This timing will allow you to fuel yourself properly yet give you enough time to digest your food adequately. An example of a prerace meal would be a banana, oatmeal, and a little peanut butter or a protein smoothie with fruit. We suggest that you do not eat anything greasy like bacon and eggs before your race. Save that for afterward.

As you are eating breakfast begin to run through your day mentally. What route are you going to take to the race? Where are you going to park? What will your warm-up routine be? You will have thought out those things before today, as you learned in the previous chapter, but now you are using them as focus items to keep you thinking about the race. Today, your body is ready; it is trained and capable of doing what you have practiced for the preceding weeks and months. Today the X factor is your mind. Begin by putting it in a framework of positivity. By focusing on the positive, you will put yourself in the right mind to overcome any issues that may arise.

Note here that before you leave your house you should apply sunscreen. Skin cancer is a real thing, and even if it is cloudy, the sun's UV rays can burn your skin. Optimal absorption of sunscreen takes about an hour, so you should be safe doing it before you leave the house. You can apply more before your race.

Traveling to Your Race

You may encounter road closures or other changes to your original travel path to the race. Many events close roads or modify traffic patterns to make your race safer. Do not worry; you will be able to navigate around these obstacles with the help of volunteers or law enforcement officers in most instances. If you ride your bike to the venue from either your home or your parked vehicle, remember to wear your bike helmet and have it strapped properly. A little known rule is that athletes can receive a penalty for riding their bikes without a properly fastened helmet before or after a race. This rule is designed to keep you safe and decrease race liability.

As you approach the venue you will likely begin to hear music and the voice of the event announcer. These two sounds are both motivating and informative. We encourage you not to wear headphones for this reason. Although you may be eager to listen to your own music, you will miss the vital information from the announcer. Information such as water temperature and wetsuit rules is given out only on the morning of the race. Any changes to the course or event schedule will also be broadcast. Most important, if you wear headphones, you will miss out on the sounds of your first event and the encouraging words of your fellow participants and supporters.

If you have already picked up your packet the day before the race, we suggest arriving at the race venue 2 hours before your race start time. The transition area closes at specific times on race day, so you'll want to have time to set up your things in the transition area with plenty of time for a bathroom break (long lines) and a warm-up. Check with the race director or event website for those times. If you need to pick up your packet on race morning, allow an extra 30 to 45 minutes in addition to the 2 hours before the race.

Locating and Setting Up
Your Transition Spot

The next few things may occur in a different order based on your specific event, but we will lay out a typical sequence here. Locate your transition spot, the small personal space where you will set up shop for the day and where you will change from discipline to discipline. A typical transition setup has the bike being hung by the saddle with the front wheel facing out. You can place a small towel on the left side (not the drivetrain side) of your bike with your cycling shoes, running shoes, hat, gel, water bottle, and so on sitting on the towel.

Transition locations will be determined in one of three ways—assigned by number, assigned by age group, or not assigned at all. If your race assigns by number, you will have no choice in where your rack is located. You are required to remain where the event places you, and you cannot change even with the consent of another athlete. If your race assigns by age group, your transition spot will be first-come, first-served on the rack. You will later find this to be one of the primary reasons that athletes arrive to races hours before they start. Where you set up on the transition rack does not really matter, but some people have a preference. Finally, a race that has no transition spot assignment is a true free-for-all. In this case you can rack anywhere you wish in the transition area. We suggest that you rack closer to the entry or exit point of the transition area for ease and flow.

One main point of protocol that we must advise you of is that you must never move another athlete's items after they are placed onto a rack. If you believe that a bike should be moved or wonder whether a wetsuit was left by mistake, you should take a specific action. First, simply ask the athlete who owns the items whether they can be moved a bit to help fit you in. Nine times out of 10 this request will solve the problem. If the athlete in question is nowhere to be found, ask a race official or event volunteer. By having a referee or neutral event volunteer assist you, you are less likely to create a problem or conflict.

Finding the Body-Marking Station

After you set up your transition spot, you will need to find the body-marking station where volunteers typically write your race number on your arms and your age on your calf. These days, many events use temporary tattoos as race numbers. If that is the case, you may have received the numbers in your race packet and applied them at home before you arrived. If your race gave you tattoos and you left them at home, not all is lost. Find a volunteer and ask whether there is a "trouble tent" (or table) to help you. This approach will also be good for other issues like forgetting your bib number or swim cap. Trust us, plenty of people need help; those who do not ask for it end up panicking.

Picking Up Your Timing Chip

Your next stop will be to pick up your timing chip if they weren't given out when you picked up your packet. Timing chips are small electronic trackers that record your race time and all your split times throughout the day. The technology has been evolving over the years, but the standard is still the chip attached to your ankle with Velcro. As soon as you get your chip, put it on your left ankle. We say the left ankle because it is then less likely to become lodged in your bike's drive train should it come loose during the race. We suggest that you put it on right away so that you do not lose it. Some races charge athletes who lose a chip. They can be as expensive, as much as $100 each.

Warming Up Before Your Race

The hope is that you have time to warm up because a proper short and sweet warm-up before the race is a perfect way to get the blood moving, calm your nerves, and avoid injury. Assuming that your race lets you take your bike out of transition (not all do), you will be able to test the gears and make sure that everything is functioning properly. Before you leave transition, set a towel or your wetsuit on the rack so that others know you are coming back. Your ride should be a short out and back of about 10 minutes. You should run through all your gears and do a few strong accelerations of 20 to 30 seconds. When you return, put your bike in the gear you want to be starting the race in and rack it. The next part of your warm-up is a run. Again, the run should be just a short shakeout to get the legs moving, no more than 10 minutes at an easy pace. Many people choose to do this in small groups, chatting it up along the way. Be sure to include a few short accelerations to goal-race pace but keep things light. When you get back from the run, set up your transition spot for the last time, put on your wetsuit (assuming you are using one), your race-issued swim cap, and your goggles. Let's head on down to the water!

If your race requires you to use a bag drop, as some do these days, stuff everything you won't be using for the race in that. For those new to the sport, a bag drop is an area where event volunteers take your bag labeled with your race number and store it safely during the race. Your cell phone, any extra clothes, postrace snack, and anything you don't want to wear during the race should go in the bag. Your cell phone should be one of the items you place in your drop bag. This is important because after you leave transition, or it closes, you likely will not be let back in until much later. This way, you will have your phone and be able to call your friends and family, snap photos, and brag all over social media about how you are now a triathlete.

RACE-DAY SUPPORT

Your family and friends can be huge race-day supporters for you. For example, maybe your best friend can get up early and drop you off at the race start so that you don't have to panic about finding a spot to park. Maybe your family will wake up at a more reasonable hour and be there to see you at the swim start and at certain distance markers on the bike and run courses holding handmade signs to cheer you on. If your parents live nearby, they can cheer you on out on the course or watch your kids while your significant other runs around on the course to give you motivation to keep going. The more people you have helping and cheering for you on race day, the better your spirits and determination will be to finish the race!

Familiarizing Yourself With the Sequence of the Race

Now that your bag is dropped, it's time to discuss the race as it will unfold. We will start with the swim start and work our way through T1, the bike, T2, the run and then the finish line. We cover what to expect, how to navigate through each aspect of the race course.

SWIM START AND SWIM COURSE

Some race venues offer a small roped-off area that allows racers to warm up with a short swim before the race start, an activity that permits you to get used to the water temperature. If you can't get in the water, try doing some jumping jacks or use swim cords to warm up and get your muscles awake for the start of the race. Race starts are usually one of three types of start formats described in chapter 5 (see the section "Choosing a Swim Start"). Position yourself based on your confidence with the swim and the format of the start.

Before the gun goes off, take a moment to look around. See the sun rising, hear the crowd cheering, and smell the weird smells that come from athletes. These little things are what make the experience so special. If you do not take a moment to breathe it in, you will regret it later when all you have as memories are split times. In addition, take a few moments to make sure that your equipment is all set. If you're wearing a wetsuit, make sure that the zipper is in the back. Put your goggles on first and then your swim cap over them so that they don't come off during the swim. If the water is cold, splash a little on your face to alleviate the initial shock that can come from your face hitting the cold water first.

Also, before the start, look at where the buoys are, what shape and color the corner ones are, and how many there are. While in the water, you should sight for the buoys every three or four strokes so that you stay on course. When going around the buoys, we suggest you stay a bit wider if you are a bronze- or silver-level swimmer. If you are a gold-level swimmer and don't mind body contact, you can go in closer to the buoys if you'd like.

During the swim, keep calm and breathe, because the swim can be a bit rough with other athletes swimming into you or over you. If for some reason you get tossed around, lose your goggles, or panic a bit, slow down, do the breaststroke, or float on your back for a few moments to catch your breath. Then continue with your swim. Kayaks, boats, and lifeguards will be in the water if you get distressed and need assistance; just yell and wave them down. Note that if you do receive assistance out of the water, you will not be allowed to continue the race on the bike or run. Safety comes first; use your best judgment.

As you approach the shore, swim in as far as you can until your fingers hit the bottom. Then get up and run through the water to T1. On your run up, you can remove your goggles and swim cap and pull your wetsuit down to your waist to speed up the T1 process. This occasion is another perfect time to breathe in the atmosphere. Look for your family and friends, high-five a kid, or simply yell, "I did it!" Either way, it's one down and two to go.

TRANSITION 1 (T1)

The swim is done! Check it off the list and get out of your wetsuit if you wore one. Hang it on the bike rack and put on the shirt or jersey you are going to wear, grab your helmet, strap it on, and then grab your sunglasses and bike shoes. If you are going to wear socks, put them on before you unrack your bike. Next, take your bike and run it out of transition to the mount line, moving over to the right before you get on your bike. You want to be safe and allow other athletes to get on their bikes, too. After you are on the bike, pedal a few times and clip in. Now get riding!

BIKE COURSE

Most of the sprint races that beginners participate in will be nondrafting races, which we talked about earlier in the book. In these events

Transition 1 (T1): Change out of your wetsuit and gather your biking gear.

USA Triathlon/Rich Cruse

you are required to keep three bike lengths back from any other athlete. Remember that not all bike courses are closed to vehicles, so always stay alert. If for some reason you happen to have a flat or mechanical issue, you will have to fix it yourself, but the good news is that you can continue the race. If you have a mechanical issue that you just can't fix, find the nearest race official or volunteer and let her or him know you need help. If it rains during the race, be sure to slow down on any descents, avoid any paint on the road, and go through corners with caution, because they can get slippery.

Again, while you are on the bike, take some time to look around. Encourage athletes who are passing you, as well as those you are passing. As you come near the end of the bike course, you should start to think about getting ready for the run. Be sure to slow down when you get within 100 yards (m) of the finish. Dynamiting the brakes at the dismount line is never a good idea and can lead to a nasty crash. Play it safe and dismount before the dismount line. After you are off your bike, run with it back into the transition area to your transition spot.

TRANSITION 2 (T2)

You have completed the bike portion of the race—way to go! Rack your back and take off your helmet and cycling shoes. Put on your running shoes, hat or visor, and your race belt and head out on the final part of the race. Be sure to look for the run out signs. As you head out, look around for your fans; they will surely be screaming for you. Give them some love and attention. Don't dilly-dally—you still have the run left— but it's now two down and only one to go.

RUN COURSE

The run can feel strange after riding. Your legs may feel slow, so start conservatively and then slowly pick up the pace. The run can be the hottest part of the race, so be sure to stay hydrated. Don't be afraid to splash some water on your face and head to stay cool. The run can also upset your stomach, especially if you accidentally swallowed a bit of water during the swim. If you do suffer from GI distress while you're running, slow down a bit, don't eat anything (you don't need to eat anything on the run during a sprint-distance race anyway), and try to work through it if you can. If things get too uncomfortable, use the porta potties that are located on the run course for most races.

Remember, in triathlon it is against the rules to run with headphones. Let the music of the day propel you forward and use the crowd as motivation. Before you know it you will hear the music from the finish line and the cheers of the crowds at the end. Put on your best smile and zip up your jersey so that you look good for finish-line photos. This photo will inevitably become your favorite one, at least until you finish your next race. Remember that you will finish your first race only once.

Transition 2 (T2): Change into your running shoes quickly.

You will never get this moment back, so drink it in and make it special. Some races allow you to cross hand in hand with a family member or child. If that is the case, grab the child's little paw and tell him or her to run like the wind. Neither of you will ever forget the experience.

Finishing the Race

Congratulations! You've crossed the finish line for your first sprint- or standard-distance race. All your training, dedication, motivation, and hard work have paid off. Wear your finisher medal with pride and celebrate with your family and friends. Take lots of photos and be sure to look around at the spectacle that is a triathlon finish. To help with recovery, get hydration and postrace nutrition into your body within 30 to 60 minutes of finishing. You can normally do this at a tent near the finish that supplies races with postrace food. Some races go all out—heck, we have even seen full Hawaiian-style luaus at the end of some races. Either way, delicious food is just one more way of making this day special for you. Be sure to consume a drink with electrolytes such as Gatorade or Powerade. Some people like to refuel with chocolate milk, but try that only if your stomach can handle it. You'll want to eat a snack with some carbohydrate and protein, so depending on the postrace food, you may want to bring some of your own. An energy bar, peanut butter and jelly sandwich, apple, and almonds are all easy to digest and pack in your car for after the race. If you have finished the race and are really hungry, go out and get a burger with your family—you've earned it. As for helping your muscles recover, you can get off your feet and enjoy a few days off. If you're lucky, your race may offer free postrace massages, which are heavenly. The bottom line is to take care of yourself. If you wake up sore the next few days after the race, you can try an easy swim or a short spin on the bike. Take it easy and give your body the rest it needs.

Congratulations! You are now a triathlete—something no one can ever take away from you. It's been an amazing journey. In our final chapter we help you assess your race. You can analyze your times, strategies, paces, photos, tan lines, and start planning for your next race!

CHAPTER 14

ASSESSING YOUR PERFORMANCE

To start this chapter and end this book, we want to tell you, "Congratulations!" Let us be the first to say that we are super proud of you and what you just accomplished. We know you are feeling a rush of mixed emotions, likely anything from pure excitement over the fact you really did it to a feeling of regret because you didn't go faster or walked too much (yes, we all walk at some point in time on the run). So how do you begin to break down your day and truly assess what you accomplished? We will take it step by step with the goal of learning, evaluating, and forming the groundwork of where you go from here.

Reflecting on Your Race

The first thing that most triathletes take away from a race is a list of times, commonly referred to as splits. We will set those aside for a moment and focus on something else entirely.

In our opinion, one of the best things you can do after a race is to reflect on what went right, what went wrong, and what went really wrong. Sooner rather than later, take a moment to write all this down because as time passes, you tend to forget details and the details are what you really want to record here. Make honest assessments and document what you did before the race:

- What and when did you eat and drink? Did these items work well for you?
- How much sleep did you get? Was it enough?
- Did you give yourself enough time to get to the race venue?
- Did your packing lists cover all your needs? Do you need to add to it or subtract from it?
- Did you pack the correct warm-up and postrace clothes?

If all these were spot on, great! If not, you need to figure something else out for next time.

Now list three things that went well or right during your day. We ask you to do this because most athletes focus on the things that went wrong. We believe in encouraging positive thinking, so we want you to think positively first. What went right could be something as simple as that you remembered to tie your shoes. That example may seem silly, but positive thinking has mental ramifications that will benefit you in the future; likewise, negative thinking can create limits to your enjoyment and success in the future. After you have written down the good stuff, you have permission to write down what could have gone better. This list can consist of things that are either in or out of your control. For example, you can say that the bike portion of the race was awful because it was cold and raining. But guess what? The conditions were the same for everyone, so let that go. Don't fixate on things that were out of your control. But if you wrote that you fell because you slipped on fresh road paint while cornering on the bike course in the rain, you have a learning point that you can use in future races. You can think about avoiding riding on paint in corners or in the rain because you know that you could fall. On your future training rides you can dip into the toolbox of knowledge you are starting to create through personal experience. Imagine each of these small events as tools in a box you will carry with you for the rest of your life. The more tools you have, the better you will be prepared to handle the same or similar situation in the future. This knowledge will increase your confidence and thus improve your performance.

Steve Lovegrove/fotolia.com

The type of start you choose—mass, wave, or time-trial —can affect your swim time during the race.

Let's assume you now are completely jazzed to do another triathlon. What about this race did you like and not like? Did the race organization inform you well enough before the event? Did you like the swag (race shirt, other give-a-ways)? Were the support and volunteers on the course friendly, helpful, and abundant? Was the topography too hilly, too curvy, or too flat? Was the swim course a good one? All these things should influence you in choosing your next races. Race directors do various things to attract athletes, from early bird pricing to fabulous postrace raffle items. Did you get a medal at the end? Many athletes like to hang these in their homes or offices. Take some time to reflect on all these things so that you can begin to plan your races going forward.

Tracking Your Numbers

Now you are ready to dive deep into your numbers. Let's first discuss what they mean and what they don't mean. You have likely been tracking your numbers during your training, so you can now begin to evaluate your segments based on your training accomplishments.

SWIM TIMES

The first split you will see is your swim split. The first thing to understand here is that swim courses are almost never the distance they claim to be. Swim courses are set using GPS, landmarks, or just by sight. When the timer sets your split speed in pace per 100 yards (m), this value may be off by any number of yards (meters) and minutes because of the incorrect distance. The second reason is that most swim exit timing mats are not located right at the water's edge. They are located closer to the transition area because of power requirements and wireless transmission needs. This placement will throw off your true swim time because it will include time running or walking after you exit the water. The best way to judge your effort in the swim is to compare your time with times of people you know who swim at a similar speed in the pool. If you beat people who are normally faster than you are in the pool, great! If the people who you normally crush beat you out of the water, you need to reexamine your open-water swim skills going into your next round of training.

Use the following points to evaluate your swim:

- Did you feel comfortable with your start? Would you change where you started in relation to the others around you? If so, make that correction.

- Did you swim straight? Did you find that you were off course when you sighted? If so, work on having a more balanced stroke in the pool or perhaps by sighting more often in the water.
- Did your goggles fog up? If so, practice using alternative methods to prevent this from occurring. Spit, commercial products, and lake or ocean water are all available options.
- Did you feel comfortable in the water? If not, you should spend some more time in open water to increase your comfort there.
- Did you drink in a bunch of water? If so, adjust your breathing so that you are exhaling more underwater and inhaling more above water.

TRANSITION 1

Transition 1 is the next split time you will see. Transition times vary from race to race. You can begin to examine your time by comparing it with that of others. As a beginner, you will no doubt get faster as you progress in your triathlon career. Transitions are one area that most people don't focus enough time on in their training. You can gain or lose significant time here, so don't dismiss it. If your time is one of the better times in the field, sweet. You have a firm grasp on it. If your time is slow, start to practice transition 1 next time you do an open-water swim. Common issues that slow down transition 1 are wetsuit issues and putting on shoes and socks. If either or both of these affected you in your race, think about what could have made these actions go smoother and faster. Record those suggested steps and practice them in your next block of training.

Use the following points to evaluate your T1:

- Did you remove your wetsuit without problems? Can you use better, or more, lubricant? Practice this every time you do an open-water swim.
- Was your gear in the location where you left it? If not, think about placing it in a different location. Remember that your bike moves, so putting items on your handlebars is not a smart move.
- Was your bike in the right gear to start the race? If not, note what gear would work best and put your bike in it before you start the swim in the next race.
- Did you get on your bike smoothly? If not, practice transitions more during your training.
- If you used clip-in pedals, did you have any issues? If so, practice clipping in and out more during your training.

BIKE TIMES

Bike courses are normally accurate when it comes to distance. If you compare your race result times to those on your bike computer, you may find that they do not match exactly, probably because your computer records information before you cross the timing mat, thus adding distance to your race. We suggest you use the timer's time and average speed because it measures a fixed distance that all athletes had to travel. If your bike computer is a GPS-based system, you should understand that GPS, although more accurate today than it was in the past, is still not 100 percent correct. Satellite acquisition and location pings can vary widely. Therefore, corners may be cut in your GPS distance, which would lead to inaccuracy. Trust the timer's split times and use those as goals for improving your bike speed in training. Take your average speed in your race and do short intervals at a 5 to 7 percent faster pace on your hard days of training. A sample workout for this purpose is to ride a 10-minute easy warm-up and then ride four 10-minute intervals just slightly faster than your average race pace. After each interval, recover with 5 minutes of easy spinning. When you are done, cool down with another 10 minutes of easy spinning followed by a solid set of stretches after you get off the bike. You need to push yourself on the hard days beyond what you are already capable of to get faster.

Use the following points to evaluate your bike:

- Did you have any mechanical issues? If not, you have done good work on your preparation and planning. If you did have problems, work on eliminating those possibilities before your next race.

- How was your cornering? Did you remember the skills we talked about in the biking chapter? Did you feel confident when you were turning? Do you need to incorporate more technique drills going forward?

- Was your cadence between 85 and 95? If not, how can you achieve average RPM in this range going forward? Do you need a better bike computer?

- Did you drink while on the bike? If you didn't, why? If you forgot to drink, do something to change that oversight like writing on your arm or on some tape that is in eyeshot on your handlebars. If you failed to drink because you were afraid of taking your hands off the handlebars, practice this skill on your future training rides. Drinking is vital to your performance and overall health.

- Did you mount and dismount adequately? If so, great! If not, spend a few practice days improving this skill.

TRANSITION 2

Transition 2 is similar to transition 1 in that it is about what you do and how fast you do it. Quick changes lead to quick times. Did you stand around a lot? If so, think about how you can change faster from the bike to the run. Could you have done some things while you were moving? Standing at your bike while you fiddle with your hat and race belt wastes time. Anything you can do while you are moving should be done moving. Less standing around means faster transition and race times.

Use the following points to evaluate your T2:

- Did you remember where your transition spot was? Doing this is sometimes easier said than done. Looking around during your setup from various points in the transition zone will help you get your bearings.

- Did you remember to take everything off and put everything on? Transition can be chaotic and can cause you to forget things. Remember to slow down and get everything done. Practicing these steps over and over during your training will help.

- Do you need to add or subtract anything from your transition gear choices? Did you really need that chair and bucket? Remember that less is better in transition.

RUN TIMES

The run is similar to the bike in that the course is normally measured accurately by the race organization. If your GPS says something different, don't rush up to a race official and complain. Recognize that your data may be flawed. Your run splits will most likely be slower than your open running race times. Experts agree that your true potential run split in a triathlon is only about 5 percent slower than your pure open running pace. Be happy in the fact that this discrepancy could mean that you have room to improve. In addition, know that the pace you held here will be a good benchmark to work from in training going forward.

Use the following points to evaluate your run:

- How was your pacing? Did you go out too hard? If you did, try to stay in more control next time.

- Did you take in enough water or nutrition? Would you drink more or less? Did you think that you had enough energy? If not, you may want to take a gel as you begin the run to get a small burst of energy.

- Did your equipment feel OK? Did you have any chafing? Did you have any problems with your shoes? Do you need to make any changes here?
- Did you smile for the cameras? Did you high-five your friends and family? Remember that these things are important as well.

TIME PENALTIES

The last thing you need to look for is to ensure you did not receive a time penalty for a rules violation. Not all races have race referees, but all races can issue time penalties if you violate one of the posted rules such as littering, unsportsmanlike conduct, or drafting. Penalties can be a tricky thing, mainly because most people do not know where the penalty sheets are posted and what the process is to appeal them. If you are unsure, ask a race volunteer or an official where the penalties are posted. If you did receive a time penalty, know that you have a short window of appeal. You will want to find a race official and inquire about the process. Penalties are rare, but most are deemed nonappealable because they are a judgement call by the referee or race official. If you were penalized, ask to have the description of the athlete and her or his clothing read to you. If this account does not describe you, you may have been penalized incorrectly. If you would like to appeal the penalty,

---

BRAGGING RIGHTS

When you go back to your place of work or business, your friends and coworkers will inevitably ask you how it went. When you start to tell your tale of the day, avoid talking about your split times. Most people will tune you out as if you were Charlie Brown's teacher. Split times are interesting to you and possibly your training buddies, but most people would rather hear about your experience. Tell them about the butterflies in your stomach, the cold and rough water, the strong wind out on the bike, and the stinky cow pasture you had to ride past twice. Tell them how beautiful the run course was and how you now have these cool new tan lines. Most people care more about how the event affected you and thus wish to hear about the experience and your reaction to it. The passion you carry for triathlon will come through in your voice. Who knows—you may recruit a new training or racing partner. Don't be afraid to say, "You should do the next one with me." If the person says something like, "I don't think I can" or "I don't know how to train," you can give them this book and they can do just what you did.

you will need to post a nonrefundable $50 cash fee upfront. You will have 30 minutes to write an appeal and deliver it to the head official. You may think that this process is cumbersome, and you are correct. It is designed specifically to limit the number of frivolous disputes that bog down the timeline of races. Essentially, if you don't litter, don't pass on the right on the bike, don't ride within three bike lengths behind a rider for an extended time on the bike (draft), don't swear at people, and are generally a good sport, you have nothing to worry about. Most races have a prerace meeting that covers the rules. We suggest that you attend these meetings to learn what not to do during your event and hear any special announcements that may be made.

We hope that your first triathlon has been an enjoyable and informative journey. We have enjoyed being a small part of it. Take time to reflect on why you chose to do the race and whether you met those desires. If you did, great. If you didn't, try it again. Many races are out there for you to choose from. Don't let this be the final chapter of your triathlon career. Keep learning. Never stop striving to be better and have more fun. Remember, triathlon is a social sport, both in training and on the field of play. Always be sure to have something good to say to others. You never know—the person to whom you say, "Keep going, you got this" just might be one of us.

GLOSSARY

Active recovery – A very easy workout intended to promote recovery from hard training.

Aerobic – A level of exertion typically defined by an effort you can sustain for more than sixty minutes.

Age group – A competitive division among the amateurs in a race, such as "male 24-29."

Age grouper – An amateur triathlete.

Aerobars – A type of bicycle handlebar that increases rider aerodynamics and reduces drag.

Aquabikes – A race format of swim and bike.

Aquathlon – A race format of run, swim, run.

Base phase – The period during a training cycle where basic endurance is the focus, normally in the beginning of a season.

Baseline fitness – The level of fitness according to the questionnaire at the beginning of the book.

Body marking – The writing of your race number and age group typically on your leg and arm with a marker or temporary tattoo.

Bonk – A term used to describe extreme exhaustion caused by a lack of carbohydrates, water, energy or a combination of all three in the body.

BOP (Back of the Pack) – A triathlete who typically finishes at or near last in a race.

Breakthrough workout – An exercise intended to be vital to the progression of an athlete's fitness.

Brick – A continuous workout which combines any two or three of the main sports of triathlon in any combination.

Bronze-level fitness – The lowest level of fitness according to the questionnaire at the beginning of the book.

Build phase – A period in training where intensity and volume are increased, normally following the base phase.

Cadence – Revolutions or cycles per minute of the swim stroke, pedal stroke, or run stride.

Cool-down – Low-intensity exercise typically at the end of a workout.

Cross-training – Training for more than one sport during a period of time.

DNF (Did Not Finish) – An abbreviation used to refer to someone who did not finish an event.

DNS (Did Not Start) – An abbreviation used to refer to someone who did not start a race they were registered for.

Drafting – Swimming, biking or running in close enough proximity behind another athlete that it reduces effort or exertion to maintain speed.

Drops – The lower portion of traditional road style bicycle handlebars.

Duathlon – A race format of run, bike, run.

Duration – The length of time of a given exercise.

Endurance – The ability to continue and resist fatigue.

Fartlek – A Swedish word meaning "speed play" also known as an un-structured interval style workout.

Fast twitch – The muscle fiber characterized by fast contraction time and most commonly associated with quick, high intensity exercises.

Free weights – Weights that are not part of an exercise machine or system, kettle-bells for example.

Frequency – The number of times per week an individual exercises.

Full Ironman – A race distance of a 2.4 mile swim, 112 mile bike, and a 26.2 mile run.

Glucose – A simple sugar.

Glycemic index – A stem of ranking carbohydrate foods based on how quickly they raise the blood's glucose levels.

Glycogen – The form in which glucose is stored in the muscles and the liver.

Gold-level fitness – The highest level of fitness according to the questionnaire at the beginning of the book.

Half-Ironman – A triathlon consisting of a 1.2 mile swim, 56 mile bike, and 13.1 mile run.

Hammer – A hard, strong, fast sustained effort.

Hamstring – The muscle located on the back of the thigh that flexes the knee and extends the hip.

Hoods – The top silicon covers of standard road bike brakes and shifters.

Intensity – The qualitative element of training referring to effort, speed, and power.

Intervals – A type of high-intensity exercise marked by short but regu-larly repeated periods of hard efforts separated by periods of recovery.

Ironman – A trademarked brand owned by the World Triathlon Corpo-ration referring to a triathlon consisting of a 2.4 mile swim, 112 mile bike, and 26.2 mile run.

ITU long-course – A race format of 1.2 mile swim, 56 mile bike, and 13.1 mile run.

Lactate – A chemical formed when lactic acid from the muscles enters the blood stream.

Mash – To cycle in a hard gear with a low cadence.

Masters – Older athletes usually over the age of 40.

MOP (Middle of the Pack) – A triathlete who traditionally finishes in the middle of the field of entrants.

Newbie – A person new to triathlon, a new triathlete.

Olympic-distance triathlon – Sometimes referred to as a "standard distance", a triathlon consisting of a 1500 meter swim, 25 mile bike and a 6.2 mile run.

Over training – A state of extreme fatigue, both physical and mental, caused by excessively training at a level higher than the body can adapt to.

Paratriathlon – Triathlon for athletes with disabilities.

Passive recovery – A period of time with no training, designed to promote recovery from intense training, a day off. (*see also* Active recovery)

Periodization – A method of sequentially organizing training to achieve a high level of fitness for a race or event.

PB (Personal Best) – A person's best result for a given swim, bike, run, or event distance. (*see also* Personal Record)

PR (Personal Record) – A person's fastest recorded time for a given swim, bike, run or event distance. (*see also* Personal Best)

Quadriceps – The large muscle in the front of the thigh that straightens the knee and flexes the hip.

Race phase – A period in training where volume and intensity are usually low allowing the athlete to compete at peak ability.

Recovery – A period of time in training where rest is assigned.

Repetition – The number of times a task, such as lifting a weight, is repeated.

RPM (Revolutions per Minute) – Cycles per minute of a single bike pedal.

Sculling – The quick movement of your palms and forearms, that create propulsion for you to stay on top of the water and also gives you the feeling and the efficiency of swim strokes.

Set – A group of repetitions.

Silver-level fitness – The middle level of fitness according to the questionnaire at the beginning of the book.

Singlet – A sleeveless shirt, often worn when running or biking.

Slow twitch – A muscle fiber characterized by slow contraction time and most commonly associated with low power and long duration exercises.

Spinning – Pedaling at a high cadence or RPM.

Split – A time for a given portion of an event.

Sprint-distance triathlon – A triathlon consisting of a 750- meter swim, 20-kilometer bike and 5 kilometer run.

Standard-distance triathlon – A race format of a 1500 meter swim, 40 km bike, and a 10 km run.

T1 – Transition number 1, typically from swim to bike.

T2 – Transition number 2, typically from bike to run.

Taper – A period of time before an event designed to have progressively decreasing intensity and volume in order to achieve top athletic performance.

Threshold – A level of exertion typically defined as the point where the body requires more oxygen than it can supply.

Training – A comprehensive program intended to prepare an athlete for an event.

Transition – An area designed for changing from one sport to another in a triathlon.

Triathlon Readiness Assessment (TRA) – An assessment to dictate the level of athlete—bronze, silver, or gold.

Tops – The portion of a bike handlebars closest to the stem.

VO$_2$max – The capacity for oxygen consumption by the body during maximal exertion.

Volume – A quantitative element of training such as miles or yards of training within a specific time period.

Warm-up – A period of gradually increased intensity of exercise designed to reduce injury during the main work out.

Wave – A group of athletes within a race who start at the same time, normally of similar age, gender, or ability.

INDEX

Note: The italicized *f* and *t* following page numbers refer to figures and tables, respectively.

ABOUT USA TRIATHLON

USA Triathlon (USAT) is the national governing body of triathlons and other multisport disciplines in the United States. The organization is the sanctioning authority for more than 4,300 diverse events ranging from grassroots to national championship races across the country. The organization works to create interest and participation through a variety of programs, including camps, clinics, races, and educational opportunities. USA Triathlon's nearly 500,000 members are coaches, race directors, officials, athletes of all ages, parents, and multisport enthusiasts, all of whom contribute to the success of the sport in the United States.

USA Triathlon is responsible for the identification, selection, and training of elite triathletes who represent the United States in international competitions, including International Triathlon Union (ITU) World Championships, Pan American Games, and the Olympic and Paralympic Games.

USA Triathlon also fosters grassroots expansion of the sport, which is facilitated by the sanctioning of age-group events and triathlon clubs around the country. In addition to local races in all 50 states, USA Triathlon hosts national and regional championships for triathletes ages 7 to 80 and older.

USA Triathlon strives to expand and inspire the triathlon community while providing the resources required for all involved to reach their potential.

ABOUT THE AUTHORS

Kris Swarthout (left) and Linda Cleveland (right)

Linda Cleveland, MS, CSCS, is a USA Triathlon Level II certified coach and the coach development senior manager at USA Triathlon. She is the editor and lead contributing author of the bestselling Complete Triathlon Guide (Human Kinetics, 2012). She has a bachelor's degree in exercise fitness management with a minor in health promotion from the University of Wisconsin–Oshkosh, along with a master's degree in exercise and wellness from Arizona State University. She has been an adjunct faculty member at Arizona State University, worked in corporate wellness at Motorola in Phoenix, and coached triathletes, cyclists, and runners since 2004.

Cleveland has been with USA Triathlon (USAT) since 2005. As the coach development senior manager, she is responsible for overseeing a variety of programs in the education department, including coaching certification clinics and curriculum, mentorship opportunities in elite coaching, performance coaching newsletters, USAT University, webinars, youth clinics, and the SafeSport program. Since joining USAT, she has made the coaching education program one of the most highly regarded in any national governing body. Cleveland offers high-performance coaches the opportunity to learn what it takes to work with world-class athletes, and she teaches new coaches how to work with beginner athletes. She has served as a head coach at several International Triathlon Union (ITU) races, including continental cups, world cups, and world championship series races.

Cleveland keeps active by training and by chasing her young son and daughter around the mountains of Colorado. She enjoys hiking, skiing, mountain biking, fishing, and enjoying time in the great outdoors.

Kris Swarthout has been a competitive presence in triathlons since 2001, first as an athlete and now as a coach. He is currently the Midwest regional chairperson for USA Triathlon, the owner of Final K Sporting Services, and the head coach of the Minnesota chapter of the Z3 Junior/Youth High Performance Team. He has been selected as age-group coach for Team USA by USA Triathlon four times and accompanied Team USA to the ITU world championships around the globe.

Swarthout has coached athletes ranging from professional to first-time amateurs. He strives to help people achieve the ultimate balance of family and sport in their lives. He coauthored the current USA Triathlon Level 1 coaches' training manual and has been published and quoted in some of the world's biggest newspapers and other media, including the New York Times, Boston Globe, Minneapolis Star Tribune, BBC, Runner's World, and Triathlete.

Making his home in Minneapolis, Minnesota, Swarthout is a USAT Level II coach, a USAT youth and junior coach, a USAT Level 1 race director, and a USA Track and Field Level 1 coach.